Tennessee

TENNESSEE
BY ROAD

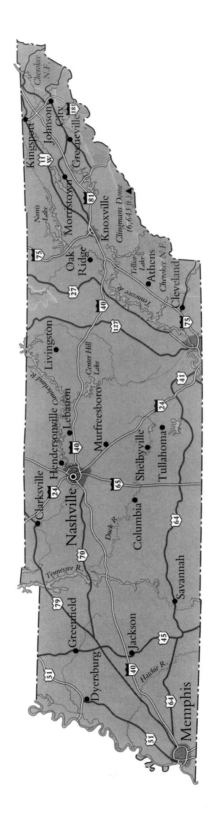

Celebrate the States

Tennessee

Tracy Barrett

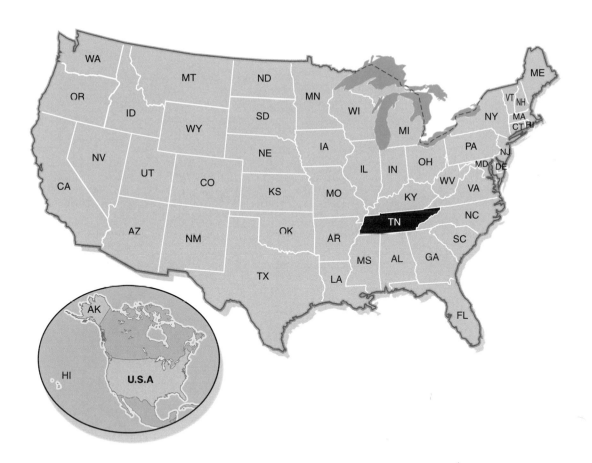

mc **Marshall Cavendish**
Benchmark
New York

For the seven-foot-tall Tennessee ridge runner

Marshall Cavendish Benchmark
99 White Plains Road
Tarrytown, NY 10591-9001
www.marshallcavendish.us

Library of Congress Cataloging-in-Publication Data
Barrett, Tracy, 1955–
Tennessee / by Tracy Barrett.—2nd ed.
p. cm. — (Celebrate the states)
Summary: "Provides comprehensive information on the geography, history, wildlife, governmental struc-
ture, economy, cultural diversity, peoples, religion, and landmarks of Tennessee"—Provided by publisher.
Includes bibliographical references and index.
ISBN-13: 978-0-7614-2151-1
ISBN-10: 0-7614-2151-3
1. Tennessee—Juvenile literature. I. Title. II. Series.
F436.3.B372006
976.8—dc22   2005024055

Editor: Christine Florie
Editorial Director: Michelle Bisson
Art Director: Anahid Hamparian
Series Designer: Adam Mietlowski
Photo research by Candlepants Incorporated

Cover Photo: Adam Jones/ Photo Researchers, Inc.

The photographs in this book are used by permission and through the courtesy of; *Corbis*: David Muench,
8, 23; Owaki-Kulla, 11, 54; Gary W. Carter, 12; Chase Swift, 13; Galen Rowell, 15; Raymond Gehman,
17, 21, 93, 115; William Manning, 26; PoodlesRock, 32; Bettmann, 33, 38(low), 42, 49, 62, 75, 81, 82;
37, 43, 46, 84, 131; Kevin Fleming, 52, 66, 89, 103, 104, 105; Morris Abernathy, 56; William A. Bake,
60; The Corcoran Gallery of Art, 68; Mathew B. Brady, 72; Reuters, 73; John Madere, 78; Bill Barksdale,
79; Dave G. Houser, 88; Tom Nebbia, 90; James L. Amos, 92, 108; Richard Cummins, 96; Gary W.
Carter, 97; Donald C. Johnson, 101; David Hosking, 111(top); Pat O'Hara, 111(lower); Gary Braasch,
119; Tami Chappell/Reuters, 121; John Springer Collection, 123, 127; Rufus F. Folkks, 132, 133. *Super-
Stock*: Edmond Van Hoorick, 18; age footstock, 98; Gala, 99; SuperStock Inc, 107; Richard Cummins,
135. *Getty Images*: Altrendo, 19; Robert Nunnington, back cover. *Smithsonian American Art Museum,
Washington DC/Art Resource, NY*: 28. *Painting by Greg Harlin, Courtesy Frank H. McClung Museum, The
University of Tennessee McClung Museum*: 30. *Tennessee State Museum, Tennessee Historical Society
Collection*: 38(top). *Title: Soon My Child Artist: Troy Anderson Permanent Collection of Cherokee Heritage
Museum and Gallery, Cherokee, North Carolina. Dr, Michael Abram & Dr. Susan M. Abram, curators/ Photo
by Mike Kesselring*: 39. *T.W. Wood Gallery and Arts Center*: 41. *AP/Wide World Photos*: 47; Mark
Humphrey, 51, 69; John Partipilo, 85; John Russell, 86. *Peter Arnold Inc*: Jochen Tack, 58, 64. *The Image
Works*: Mark Godfrey, 76; Jeff Greenberg, 95.

Printed in China
1 3 5 6 4 2

Contents

Tennessee is beautiful country . . .

"I've lived near the Alps and I've vacationed on the Riviera, and I think Tennessee is prettier than either of those places. It's a friendlier kind of beauty, more welcoming."

—Swiss native Monique Frank

"The greenest state in the land of the free."

—theme song from 1950s television show *Davy Crockett*

"The fairest land
From God's own hand
Is the Basin of Tennessee."

—traditional song

"When civilization first peeped over the Alleghenies and looked down upon the gorgeous landscape below, I think she shouted . . . , Lo, this is Paradise regained!"

—Tennessee governor Robert L. Taylor, 1889

. . . with friendly people . . .

"Everybody is smiling and is saying, 'Hello! How are you?' It's nice people."

—German tourist in Nashville

. . . who love their state.

"The Tennessee pioneer can be exceeded by none in fondness for and admiration of his own country. . . . In all his wanderings, his thoughts are turned constantly upon Tennessee."

—historian James G. M. Ramsey

"There's only one place worth living in, and that's Middle Tennessee. When I get out [of the military] . . . I'm going to marry a Nashville gal. I'm going to buy some Middle Tennessee land and raise Tennessee walking horses and Tennessee babies."

—homesick Tennessee soldier, 1960

"This is paradise. It's the most beautiful place I've ever seen."

—Tennessee newcomer Mary Bell

"I can't see why anyone would want to live anywhere else."

—Tennessee native Martin Miller

"We are talking now of summer evenings in Knoxville, Tennessee, in the time that I lived there so successfully disguised to myself as a child. . . . There was still daylight, shining softly and with a tarnish like the lining of a shell; and the carbon lamps lifted at the corners were on in the light, and the locusts were started, and the fireflies were out, and a few frogs were flopping in the dewy grass . . . from low in the dark . . . the regular yet spaced noises of the crickets, each a sweet cold silver noise, threenoted, like the slipping each time of three matched links of a small chain."

—James Agee, *Knoxville: Summer 1915*

What is it about Tennessee that makes Tennesseans love their state so deeply? Is it the natural beauty? The dynamic and independent people? The exciting things to do? Let's explore Tennessee and find out!

Chapter One

Seven States, or One—or Three?

The State of Tennessee has been known by at least seven different names and has had several different governments each time (the Watauga Association, 1772–1777; the Washington District, 1777–1780; the Cumberland Compact, 1780–1784; the State of Franklin, 1784–1788; the Government South of the Holston and French Broad Rivers, 1788–1790; the Territory South of the Ohio River, 1790–1796; and the State of Tennessee, 1796–present). The special Tennessee twenty-five cent piece shows three musical instruments: a banjo, representing the blue-grass music that was born in East Tennessee and in Kentucky; a guitar, standing for the country music that has made Nashville and Middle Tennessee famous around the world; and a trumpet, representing the Memphis blues of the western part of the state.

The Cumberland Gap, the gateway to the West, was formed by wind and water, creating a break in the Appalachian Mountains.

Why three instruments? Tennessee's constitution of 1834 divided the state into three "grand divisions" based on the geography of the area. The three stars on the flag of Tennessee stand for these grand divisions: East, Middle, and West.

These differences can be traced back to the forces that shaped the land. Millions of years ago Tennessee was covered by ocean. Over millions of years, pieces of the earth's surface, called tectonic plates, rubbed against each other and rose up from the ocean. Their great ridges formed the Appalachian Mountains, which run down the eastern section of the United States, from Canada to Alabama and through eastern Tennessee. The land to the west was not as disturbed by the collision of these great plates, so Middle Tennessee is a land of gentle hills, while in the west, the hills flatten out into wide plains leading to the Mississippi River.

Tennessee is shaped like a parallelogram. Only thirty-fourth of the fifty states in land area, the state is almost four times as wide as it is tall. If you were to stand in the northeastern corner of Tennessee, you would be closer to Canada than to the southwestern corner of the state!

Tennessee borders Kentucky and Virginia to the north; North Carolina to the east; Georgia, Alabama, and Mississippi to the south; and to the west, across the Mississippi River, Arkansas and Missouri. It stands at the crossroads of the North and South, and of the East and West United States.

WILD TENNESSEE

Much of Tennessee is covered by forests of deciduous (hardwood) trees, such as oak, maple, beech, and walnut, which lose their leaves in a spectacular display of color each fall. In all parts of the state, small mammals such as opossums, raccoons, bobcats, foxes, and rabbits thrive. Among the large wild animals left in Tennessee are black bears, white-tailed deer, and wild boars.

More than 150 species of trees are native to Tennessee.

A black bear takes a nap in the Great Smoky Mountains National Park.

Tennessee's 390 varieties of birds include most of those found in the rest of the United States, with quails, martens, and ravens especially common. One hundred seventy-five of these bird species nest in the state; the others merely pass through.

As humans take over more and more of the land in Tennessee, wild animal encounters are becoming more frequent. Coyotes have been spotted in built-up areas such as Nashville, foraging for garbage and eating squirrels and even cats and small dogs.

Even larger animals are venturing into populated parts of the state. For several years people living in Robertson County in Middle Tennessee wondered about a mystery animal that a local newspaper called the Carr's Creek Critter. It screamed at night, and in the morning farmers occasionally found sheep that had been killed and partially eaten. The mystery of the "critter" was solved recently when some state residents and park visitors sighted cougars (also known as mountain lions or pumas) in the area. Some appear relaxed at the sight of humans. "I . . . came within fifty feet of a large, tawny cat that was sunning on a rock near the stream," recalls one man who was taking a walk with his family. "Its body was about three feet in length, not counting the long tail. . . . He seemed only mildly startled when he realized I was there, and he looked at me for a brief second before jumping off the rock and running away. I remember its movement being very sinuous and smooth."

A small population of eastern cougars make their home in the Great Smoky Mountain National Park region. Some have even made their way into more populated areas of Tennessee.

Tennessee's abundant rivers and streams are home to many types of fish. In some areas development and pollution from industry have hurt the fish population, but at least one is making a comeback after nearly being wiped out locally due to overfishing, sediment runoff from farming, and pollution: the sturgeon. This fish can live to be one hundred years old and can reach over three hundred pounds! Scientists have reintroduced young sturgeon into the French Broad, Holston, and Tennessee rivers and are eagerly waiting to see what will happen in another fifteen or twenty years, when the fish are old enough to begin reproducing.

Environmentalists work all the time to protect the animals and plants native to Tennessee. A group known as Southern Appalachians Biodiversity Project, based in North Carolina, got the United States Fish and Wildlife Service (USFWS) to protect the habitats of thirteen endangered mussels (a kind of shellfish) and two plant species found in Tennessee, Virginia, and Alabama. The USFWS later removed the "endangered" label from one of the species, but the rest of these rare natives of the area are being protected.

All of Tennessee is covered in flowers. One expert has said that there is "a larger number of flowers and ferns thriving in Tennessee than anywhere else in the world in an equal area." These wildflowers include small but colorful specimens such as bloodroot, trilliums, and goldenseal. The showier and beautiful dogwood and redbud trees, as well as the rhododendron that flourish in eastern Tennessee, are foreign imports that have made a new home in the mild climate.

The climate in most of Tennessee is mild. Winters last longer in the hilly east, while the middle and western parts of the state have longer, more humid summers. In the spring frequent thunderstorms and occasional tornadoes threaten. In 1998 a tornado ripped through downtown Nashville and the surrounding area, destroying homes and businesses, uprooting trees

Early spring hosts a spectacular wildflower show throughout Tennessee.

planted over one hundred years earlier by President Andrew Jackson, and disrupting life in the area for months. Fortunately, the loss of life was small, and Nashville has since improved its tornado-warning system.

EASTERN MOUNTAINS AND CAVES

The hills in the eastern third of Tennessee are so steep that roads have to wind among them rather than cut straight across them. The Unaka Mountains, which make up the western edge of the Blue Ridge Range of the Appalachians, cover East Tennessee. Most of Tennessee's 13.6 million acres of forest lie in the east. These huge forests provide habitat for wildlife and income for the state in the form of timber.

Most of the rock under the mountains is limestone. Over time limestone dissolves in water, and the many underground streams in the area have carved out some huge caves. More than seven thousand caves have been discovered in Tennessee, and about two hundred more are found every year.

In the southeastern region of the state lies Lost Sea Caverns. This is the world's largest underground lake, covering 4.5 acres. Visitors can hike the three hundred feet down to the lake and ride in glass-bottomed boats to see rainbow trout and other unusual animals and rock formations.

East Tennessee's Cumberland Caverns, at twenty-eight miles long, is the largest cave system in the state and among the largest in the world. Early settlers excavated some rooms of the cave and made shelters in them. Humans weren't its only residents, though. Many contain jaguar and bear skeletons. Rats, beetles, and small mammals such as raccoons still live there, as do many salamanders.

In the nineteenth century people who explored the cave system often left their signatures on its walls and ceilings, writing them in the soot

A visitor views the Pipe Organ rock formation at Cumberland Caverns.

made by smoky torches. After the Civil War the cave system and the area around it became a popular picnicking spot.

Today, people come from all over the country to explore the caves of Tennessee. "Caving isn't for everyone," says Greg Giles of Nashville. "It is dark and wet. There are many times when you have to lie down on your stomach and just inch along, and sometimes you even have to take off your helmet and push it in front of you and turn your head sideways so you can scoot through a very low place."

Not just cavers, but archaeologists, too, are exploring East Tennessee. In 2004 a group of archaeologists from the University of Tennessee began digging up a cabin in Cades Cove inside Great Smoky Mountain National Park. It was built by an early settler named John Oliver. Members of the university's Smoky Mountain Archaeological Field School hope that the nails, broken pottery, glass, and flakes of stone they find will help them learn more about the European Americans' relationship with Native Americans in that area.

West of the Unakas is the Great Valley of East Tennessee, a 9,200-square-mile segment of the Appalachian Mountain valley that runs from New York to central Alabama. The Great Valley is an agricultural center. There tobacco, grain, and many fruits are grown, and cattle are raised.

In East Tennessee the Appalachians rise so high that their climate is more like that of Canada than that of the rest of the southern United States. Most of the trees are conifers, such as pines, that can survive in the cold. The Great Smoky Mountains in the Appalachians are covered with pines, and almost 14,000 varieties of plants (4,000 of them flowering) thrive there. One of the most spectacular is the wild tiger lily, which can grow to be six feet high. The Smokies are filled with spectacular wild rhododendron, which burst into red, pink, and white flowers in the spring. Roan Mountain has one rhododendron grove that covers more than six hundred acres!

Rich fertile land in the Great Valley produces hearty crops and provides pastures for cattle to graze.

Every June Roan Mountain bursts into color as a sea of rhododendron bloom pink and lavender.

MUD GLYPH CAVE

In 1980 some amateur spelunkers, or cave explorers, asked a farmer's permission to explore the cave on his land in southeastern Tennessee. Another caver had told them that he had found strange markings, obviously made by humans, deep inside a cavern. This cave became known as Mud Glyph Cave (a glyph is a symbol that gives information without using words).

After wiggling flat against the ground through a passage called a belly-crawl, the spelunkers hiked along an underground stream before reaching a small room where they found the glyphs.

Many late prehistoric Native Americans thought of caves as sacred, holy places and explored deep into them to find rooms to use for religious ceremonies. Anthropologists think the glyphs were drawn between the twelfth and eighteenth centuries. Some of them show no real shape; they are squiggles drawn with all the fingertips of one hand. Others are pictures of animals—a snake, an owl, and a hawk. There are also simple stick figures. One of these seems to be running with its mouth open and arms thrown up in the air, as if in fear.

THE MIDDLE: ROLLING HILLS AND PLAINS

When you have passed through the Great Valley and reached the Cumberland Plateau, you have arrived in Middle Tennessee. Although you are fairly high up, the ground around you is almost as flat as a huge tabletop. This plateau is part of the Appalachian Highlands. The soil is too sandy for growing most crops, but the rivers and streams of the plateau are great for canoeing.

Continuing west, you descend into the Central Basin, home of Nashville, the state's capital and second-largest city. This is a fertile area of gently rolling hills where farmers grow grain, hay, and vegetables. The famous Tennessee Walking Horses graze in the large, fertile meadows.

The Tennessee Walking Horse is the first breed of horse to carry a state name.

LAND AND WATER

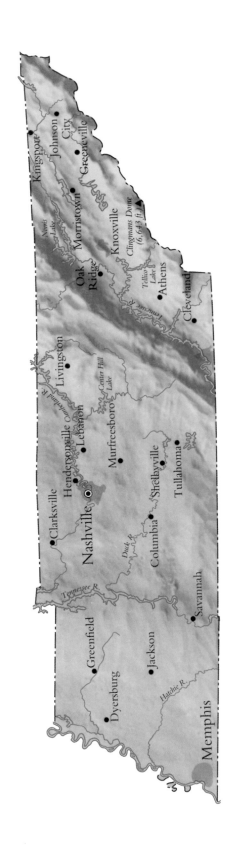

The edge of the basin is called the Highland Rim. Tobacco and cotton are grown there, and minerals such as iron are mined. The beautiful hardwood forests supply oak, ash, hickory, and cedar for buildings and furniture.

WESTERN PLAINS AND SWAMPS

Even farther west you'll find yourself in the Gulf Coastal Plain and the floodplains of the Mississippi River, where the heat, humidity, and flat land make cotton a very important crop.

You'll also find Reelfoot, Tennessee's only natural lake. The shallow waters of the lake have been called America's greatest natural fish hatchery. With water no more than six to eight feet deep in most of the lake, Reelfoot is an ideal home for fish. This abundance of fish has attracted many waterbirds that feed on them, such as egrets, herons, and anhinga. More than 250 kinds of birds live or pass through the area.

Cypress trees thrive in the shallow water. The cypress has long, skinny roots that rise out of the water, forming a structure like a cage, with the trunk perched on top. These roots hold the tree upright in the mud at the bottom of the lake.

Reelfoot Lake, an 18,000-acre natural area, is noted for its wildlife, including its cypress trees.

THE BIRTH OF REELFOOT LAKE

Reelfoot, the only natural lake in Tennessee, was named for a Native American leader whose deformed foot caused him to walk crookedly, or reel. The lake was formed during a series of strong earthquakes in 1811 and 1812. The tremors could be felt for hundreds of miles and even made church bells ring in faraway Boston, Massachusetts!

The earth split open, and a deep depression was formed near the Mississippi River. This caused the mighty river to flow backward for about fifteen minutes, until it had filled the gully. When the river returned to its normal course, it left behind a wide, shallow lake.

Eliza Bryan, a newly arrived resident of the area, described the quake:

The Mississippi first seemed to recede from its banks, and its waters gathered up like a mountain, leaving for a moment many boats, which were on their way to New Orleans, on the bare sand, in which time the poor sailors made their escape from them.

Then rising fifteen or twenty feet perpendicularly and expanding, as it were, at the same time, the banks overflowed with a retrograde current rapid as a torrent. The boats, which before had been left on the sand, were now torn from their moorings and suddenly driven up a little creek, . . . to a distance . . . of nearly a quarter of a mile.

Western Tennessee is the site of the state's largest city, Memphis, and the lowest point in the state, Shelby County. The lowlands often stay wet for long periods. Before modern medicine, the heat and humidity combined to make this an unhealthy area in which to live. In 1878 yellow fever, carried by swamp-loving mosquitoes, killed 5,152 people in Memphis.

AN APPEALING BEAUTY

Since the last ice age Tennessee's beauty and comfortable climate have beckoned to settlers. The state has few extremes of hot or cold temperatures (the average temperature is 60 degrees Fahrenheit), although the mountainous east can have occasional hard winters, and the steamy atmosphere around the Mississippi River makes the west uncomfortable in midsummer.

Tennessee ranks in the bottom third of the states in area but sixteenth in population, with close to 6 million inhabitants and over three hundred incorporated cities. More than 64 percent of Tennesseans live in cities and towns of more than 2,500 people. Many smaller communities have colorful names, such as Bucksnort, Lovely City, Only, Red Boiling Springs, Stupidville, Frog Jump, Nosey Valley, and even Nameless.

Tennessee often ranks worst or second worst of all fifty states in air quality. In its eagerness to attract new business, the state legislature has refused to pass tough laws against pollution, and many of the once-beautiful streams of the east are among the most polluted in the country.

Tennesseans are strongly attached to their home state and are increasingly aware of the damage that human activity causes to the environment. They began demanding more environmental regulations in the 1980s and 1990s. Today new laws that protect the streams, wildlife, and air of Tennessee seek to undo some of the previous damage.

Tennessee's natural beauty abounds. The state takes great pride in protecting its flora and fauna.

UTOPIAN COMMUNITIES

Tennessee's natural beauty and pleasant climate have attracted many people who wanted to start a new way of life. A British writer named Frances Wright founded a community called Nashoba in 1826 to show how freed slaves could run a successful farm. Unfortunately, she knew little about farming, and the farm failed. In 1880 the community of Rugby was set up to provide a home for young Englishmen whose older brothers had inherited their parents' property, leaving the subsequent sons homeless. Rugby is still a tourist attraction, but a typhoid fever epidemic scared off most settlers in 1881. More recently, Steve and Ina Mae Gaskin set up a communal farm (called simply The Farm) in Summertown, Tennessee, in 1971. The Farm is the only one of these experimental settlements to succeed and is still thriving.

Tennesseans' loyalty to their beautiful state is the butt of an often-told joke. A newcomer to heaven asks, "Who are all those people chained to trees?" Saint Peter replies, "Those are Tennesseans. It's Friday, and we have to chain them to keep them from going back home for the weekend."

Chapter Two

A Remarkable History

Tennessee celebrated its two-hundredth birthday as a state on June 1, 1996, but people have been living in Tennessee for more than 13,000 years. That was when the first Native Americans entered the region in pursuit of mastodons and other game animals as the glaciers melted at the end of the last ice age.

Early Native Americans left behind some mysterious remains: large mounds. One of the largest is Old Stone Fort, near Manchester in south-central Tennessee. This massive construction, built almost two thousand years ago, has dirt walls twenty feet thick that are covered with stone. Pinson Mound, in Madison County, is more than seventy feet high and the second-tallest Indian mound in the United States.

When the first European settlers arrived in Tennessee in the sixteenth century, about ten thousand Native Americans were living there. The major tribes were the Creeks, Shawnee, Yuchi, and, most numerous of all, the Cherokee, who called themselves Ani-Yunwiya, the Real People.

The region that is now Tennessee attracted peoples by its vast diversity in land, climate, rivers, plant, and animal life.

In the early 1700s the Cherokee, who were ferocious fighters, forced the Creeks and Yuchi out of East Tennessee. Some Yuchi warriors, trapped on the banks of the Hiwassee River in East Tennessee, were so terrified of being captured by the Cherokee that they massacred their own people and committed suicide to avoid falling into the hands of their enemies. By the mid-1700s the Cherokee and their spin-off group, the Chickamauga, were the only tribes left in Tennessee, with about 22,000 people living in eighty towns.

About 13,000 years ago, Tennessee's native peoples lived off the land gathering plants and shellfish for food in addition to hunting game.

In every town was a main council house where the tribal leaders met to perform religious and official functions. This house was often large enough to seat five hundred people. Each tribe was divided into seven clans (groups of people who are related to one another). The council houses had seven sides so that each of the clans could be seated together.

Cherokee society was matrilineal, meaning that children belonged to their mother's clan. Before the arrival of white settlers, some of the most important Cherokee leaders were women.

THE RABBIT AND THE TAR WOLF: A CHEROKEE TALE

Once there was such a long spell of dry weather that there was no more water in the creeks and springs. The animals held a council to discuss what to do about it. They decided to dig a well and all agreed to help, except Rabbit, who was a lazy fellow. He said, "I don't need to dig for water. The dew on the grass is enough for me."

The others did not like this, but they went to work together and dug their well. They noticed that Rabbit kept sleek and lively, although it was still dry weather and the water in the well was getting low. They said, "That tricky Rabbit steals our water at night."

So they made a wolf out of pine gum and tar and set it up by the well to scare the thief. That night Rabbit came, as he had been coming every night, to drink enough to last him all the next day. He saw the strange black object by the well and said, "Who's there?"

The tar wolf said nothing. Rabbit came nearer, but the wolf never moved. So Rabbit grew braver and said, "Get out of my way, or I'll strike you." Still the wolf never moved. Rabbit came up and struck it with his paw. The gum held his foot, and it stuck fast.

Now Rabbit was angry and said, "Let me go, or I'll kick you." Still the wolf said nothing. Then Rabbit struck again with his hind foot so hard that it was caught in the gum, and he could not move. And there he stuck until the animals came for water in the morning. When they found out who the thief was, they had great sport over him for a while and then got ready to kill him. One proposed cutting off his head. This, Rabbit said, would be useless because it had been tried before without hurting him. Other methods were proposed for killing him, all of which Rabbit said would be useless. At last it was proposed to let him loose to perish in a thicket. Upon hearing this, Rabbit pretended great uneasiness and pled hard for his life. His enemies, however, refused to listen, and he was let loose in the thicket. As soon as he was out of reach, he gave a whoop, and bounding away, exclaimed, "This is where I live!"

The first Europeans to set foot in Tennessee were the Spanish. In 1540 the explorer Hernando de Soto called the area around the Tennessee River "a wilderness, having many pondy places, with thick forests [and] some basins and lakes." English and French explorers followed in 1673.

The Europeans were delighted with what they found. The land was beautiful and fertile, and the woods and fields were full of bison and elk. But there were difficulties, too. Wolves and cougars preyed on precious livestock. In addition, most of the Cherokee were furious about the invasion of the land.

In 1540 Spanish explorers were the first Europeans to set foot in Tennessee. Later, France and England would both claim the region for themselves.

One leader who tried to keep settlers away was Tsu-gun-sini (Dragging Canoe). He was bitterly opposed to white settlement in Tennessee and refused to sign treaties with white people. His Chickamauga warriors fiercely attacked the earliest settlers.

Yet white explorers continued to come. John William Gerhard de Brahm said in 1756, "Should this country once come into the hands of the Europeans, they may with propriety call it the American Canaan [Paradise]." But only the hardiest could bear the rugged frontier life. The early trailblazers earned the name "long hunters," since they survived such a long time in the wilderness.

An entry in the journal of the explorer Pierre de Charlevoix from 1721 reads, "The country is delightful. . . . As to the forests, which almost entirely cover this immense country, there is, perhaps, nothing in nature comparable to them." But beauty was not usually a strong enough draw. Explorers had other reasons to make the difficult journey to this area. Some were looking for a passage westward across the Appalachians. This was accomplished in 1775, when the long hunter Daniel Boone helped clear the Cumberland Gap.

In 1775 Daniel Boone and a party of settlers established the Cumberland Gap, a route used by thousands during their westward migration.

CUMBERLAND GAP

The Cumberland Mountains are part of the Appalachian Mountain Range, which extends from Pennsylvania to Alabama. The Cumberland Gap, located where Tennessee, Virginia, and Kentucky meet, is a deep pass in the mountains that served as one of the main pathways by which the early settlers were able to move westward. Daniel Boone, noted backwoodsman, trapper, and Indian fighter, helped clear the gap in 1775.

The first white man in Cumberland Gap,
The first white man in Cumberland Gap,
The first white man in Cumberland Gap,
Was Doctor Walker, an English chap.

Cumberland Gap is a noted place,
Cumberland Gap is a noted place,
Cumberland Gap is a noted place,
Three kinds of water to wash your face.

Daniel Boone on Pinnacle Rock,
Daniel Boone on Pinnacle Rock,
Daniel Boone on Pinnacle Rock,
He killed bears with his old flintlock.

Cumberland Gap, with its cliffs and rocks,
Cumberland Gap, with its cliffs and rocks,
Cumberland Gap, with its cliffs and rocks,
Home of the panther, bear, and fox.

Me and my wife and my wife's grandpap,
Me and my wife and my wife's grandpap,
Me and my wife and my wife's grandpap,
We all live in Cumberland Gap.

The majority of Europeans came to the area to build a new and free life. The first city in Tennessee was Jonesborough, founded in 1779 in the eastern part of the state. Fort Nashborough, later called Nashville, was established that same winter by James Robertson and John Donelson. The settlement grew slowly. Lewis Brantz's 1785 journal noted that "Nashville is a recently founded place and contains only two houses . . . the rest are only huts."

Most settlers lived in log cabins with just one room and wooden floors. Travel was difficult. Francis Baily, an Englishman who visited Tennessee in the 1790s, said of a tavern, "There were three or four beds of the roughest construction in one room, which was open at all hours of the night for the reception of any rude rabble that had a mind to put up at the house; and if the other beds happened to be occupied, you might be surprised when you awoke in the morning to find a bed fellow by your side whom you had never seen before, and might never see again."

Near Norris in East Tennessee is the Museum of Appalachia, one of the world's largest and most authentic historic parks, which is dedicated to representing the early history of the settlers in Tennessee. There visitors can see dozens of reconstructed log cabins and many artifacts from the hills: farm implements, household items, and toys. Local people demonstrate crafts common to the region, such as basket weaving and whittling.

THE PATH TO STATEHOOD

The American colonies declared their independence from Great Britain in 1775. The Revolutionary War was fought to defend this independence. Though Tennessee was not a separate colony, its residents took action when the British tried to take control of the "overmountain" territories, which included what is now Tennessee. One thousand Tennesseans went to fight with the Americans in South Carolina. They helped win one of the war's most important conflicts, the Battle of Kings Mountain, in 1780.

After the war Tennessee became part of North Carolina. Then in 1784, the East Tennesseans broke away and formed a new independent state, the State of Franklin (named for Benjamin Franklin). They elected John Sevier governor; but after his term ended in 1788 Franklin rejoined North Carolina.

The Battle of Kings Mountain was fought by many Tennessee Overmountain Men.

In 1790 Tennessee became the Territory South of the River Ohio. Most residents were happy, when in 1796, the population reached 77,000, which was enough for the territory to apply for statehood. Tennessee was made the sixteenth state, the first state created from a territory. Knoxville was its capital, and the popular John Sevier became its first governor.

John Sevier served as Tennessee's first governor from 1796 to 1801 and again from 1803 to 1809.

THE TRAIL OF TEARS

In 1812 the United States once again went to war with England. So many Tennesseans volunteered to fight that the state earned the nickname the Volunteer State. Tennessee's Andrew Jackson became one of the greatest heroes of the War of 1812. He would go on to be elected president of the United States in 1828 and again in 1832.

Jackson acted ruthlessly against the Native Americans, both as a soldier and as president. Davy Crockett, who fought with Jackson, later said that under Jackson's command, Native Americans were shot "like dogs."

It was Jackson who ordered the Cherokee and other native people to be removed to land west of the Mississippi River. Some of the Tennessee Cherokee managed to hide from the soldiers who were rounding them up, and their descendants now live in East Tennessee. The white people called this forced march in the harsh winter of 1838–1839 The Indian Removal, but it is better known today by the Cherokee name: the Trail of Tears.

Andrew Jackson, the seventh president of the United States, was the first man elected from Tennessee to the House of Representatives.

The painting Soon My Child, *by Troy Anderson, depicts the hardships endured by the Cherokee on their enforced move to the west of the Mississippi River.*

Many Native Americans as well as white people fought in vain to prevent this brutal action. A general who was ordered to force the Cherokee off their lands told his soldiers to disobey, saying he refused to carry out "at the point of the bayonet a treaty made by a lean minority against the will and authority of the Cherokee people."

But Jackson's will ultimately prevailed. Soldiers rounded people up in a brutal action. They seized children in the fields and then held them to tempt their parents out of hiding. A white observer said, "The parting scene was more moving than I was prepared for; when this hour of leave-taking arrived I saw many a manly cheek suffused [covered] with tears. Parents were turning with sick hearts from children who were about to seek other homes in a far off and stranger land; and brothers and sisters with heaving bosoms and brimful eyes were wringing each others' hands for the last time."

The Native Americans slowly made their way across the country, traveling on foot and by flatboat. One observer of their passage saw in their faces "a downcast defeated look bordering upon the appearance of despair." Of the 17,000 Native Americans forced to leave their ancestral lands, at least 4,000 (some estimate as many as 8,000) died by the time the Cherokee reached their final destination in Oklahoma.

Today, the Cherokee Nation is divided into two parts: the Western Band, headquartered in Tahlequah, Oklahoma, and the Eastern Band, based in North Carolina, close to its border with Tennessee. Over ten thousand members of the Cherokee Nation live in the Eastern Band, and every year since 1950, they have put on a play dramatizing the events that led to the brutal Trail of Tears.

FROM SLAVERY TO CIVIL WAR

At this time much of Tennessee was still sparsely populated. Alexis de Tocqueville, a French visitor to the United States, lamented in his 1831 book *Journey to America,* "After Nashville, not a town on the way. Nothing but a few villages, scattered here and there, all the way to Memphis." Farmers scratched out a living in these areas. Many of those who were working the hardest were slaves.

Most black Tennesseans lived in slavery. In the early nineteenth century some white people, especially in the eastern part of the state, formed societies that supported the freeing of slaves, but most of them had given up by the 1830s. The Constitutional Convention of 1834 took away free blacks' right to vote (slaves had never had it). In 1840 slaves accounted for 183,057 Tennesseans, and only about 5,000 of the blacks living in the state were free.

Disagreements over the rights of states to decide certain matters, among the most important the legality of slavery, led eleven southern states to secede

Several regions in Tennessee were against slavery from as early as 1819. However, farmers in other areas owned slaves to work their land.

(remove themselves) in 1860–1861 from the United States. The people of Tennessee had a hard time agreeing on whether to secede. It has been said that "Tennessee's head was with the Union, but her heart was with the South." When the Civil War broke out, Tennessee joined the Confederacy in 1861. Scott County, in pro-Union East Tennessee, promptly seceded from Tennessee and did not officially rejoin the state until 1986.

More Civil War battles were fought in Tennessee than in any other state except Virginia. One of the bloodiest combats of the entire war took place in the West Tennessee town of Shiloh in 1862, during which 23,500 men

The Battle of Shiloh lasted for two days, resulting in the defeat of the Confederate army.

were killed. The Battle of Shiloh shocked the nation. In this one conflict more soldiers were killed than in all three wars that had been fought on American soil before that day (the Revolutionary War, the War of 1812, and the Mexican War) combined.

The peaceful fields erupted in smoke and the crack of rifles. Children who went out to play in the morning could not make their way home through the bloodshed. When they did, they found a path covered with dead and dying soldiers, many farmhouses damaged, and their families either dead or in flight from the marauding armies.

Carol Hamlett, who grew up in nearby Crockett County, says of the battlefield, "For anyone who has any sense of history, the place is so peaceful, yet so somber. It's all still there. There isn't any big city nearby to take over the land, so you can still see the fields and orchards the way they were when the battle was being fought."

Twenty thousand black Tennesseans fought in the Civil War, most of them on the Union side. In the last important conflict in the state, the Battle of Nashville (December 1864), more than 15 percent of the soldiers in the front lines were black. "The blood of white and black men has flowed freely together," said the Union general George Thomas, "for the great cause which is to give freedom."

The Civil War divided Tennessee as it did no other state. Many thousands of its citizens fought for the Confederacy, and many fought for the Union in 1866. When the war was over, Tennessee, the last state to join the Confederacy, was the first to rejoin the Union.

The war shattered the state. A visitor said in 1863, "In happier days, Nashville must have been a very pleasant dwelling-place; but when I saw it, the whole aspect of the city was, even for a stranger, a dreary and dismal one. . . . [It looked] like a city still stunned by the blow of some great public calamity."

This illustration depicts new African-American recruits boarding railroad cars for Murfreesboro, Tennessee, to join the Federal army in 1863.

A WOMAN WITH A MISSION

Most Americans know about Paul Revere, who rode twelve miles to warn the colonists that the redcoats were coming at the start of the American Revolution. But how many have heard about the Tennessee woman Mary Love, who rode thirty-five miles through enemy territory on an equally dangerous mission during the Civil War?

The Union general Ulysses S. Grant needed to send a message to General Ambrose Burnside in Knoxville. So risky was this mission that he sent five different messengers by five different routes, hoping that at least one of them would make it. When one courier stopped, exhausted, at the Love home in Kingston, Mary hid the message in her clothes, leaped onto a horse, and galloped off toward Knoxville.

She was caught by the enemy and taken in for questioning but did not give up any information—unlike Paul Revere! They released her, and she continued on to her brother's home in Knoxville, arriving there too exhausted to finish the journey. A thirteen-year-old boy took the message the rest of the way.

REBUILDING

The end of the Civil War did not mean the end of racial troubles in Tennessee. In 1865 the Ku Klux Klan, a white supremacist group, was formed in Pulaski, Tennessee. One of its earliest leaders was the former Confederate general Nathan Bedford Forrest. Forrest had been a slave trader in

Memphis before becoming a soldier. The Klan tried to keep blacks from voting (a right they were granted in 1867) and from assuming other civil rights. The Klan was outlawed in 1869.

Reconstruction (the post-Civil War era) was very hard on Tennessee. The economy was ruined. Many farms had been severely damaged, and crops and livestock had been taken by soldiers. The North was bitter toward its former enemy, and much of the South did not trust the state that had been drawn so reluctantly into the Confederacy.

Still, the state began to rebuild itself slowly. Tennesseans realized the importance of education in helping their state rebound from the disastrous war. School reforms began immediately after the Civil War. Even the Tennessean Andrew Johnson, who became the U.S. president after Abraham Lincoln was assassinated, had not known how to read until his wife taught him. Clearly, something had to be done. A public school system for whites was established in 1867, although separate public schools for black children did not open until 1909. The school system grew slowly. By 1872 fewer than one-fifth of the state's children had access to education. Fisk, a university originally intended for black students, was founded in 1866 in a former Union army hospital. And in 1873 the New York millionaire Cornelius Vanderbilt gave $1 million to Vanderbilt University to help the healing process between North and South.

STRUGGLING FOR EQUAL RIGHTS

One of the most bitter fights of early-twentieth-century America was over women's right to vote. In order for women to gain this right, the U.S. Constitution had to be amended, or changed. Thirty-six states had to ratify (approve) this amendment for it to become law. By a narrow majority in 1920, Tennessee became the thirty-sixth state to ratify the amendment.

Campaigns to encourage women to go to the polls, such as Rock the Vote, have helped turn the tide: while in 1996 a smaller percentage of women in Tennessee voted in the national election than in any other state in the country, by 2004 more Tennessee women voted than in many other states.

A banner is unfurled from the balcony of the National Women's Party headquarters in Washington, D.C., celebrating women's right to vote in Tennessee.

MOTHER KNOWS BEST

Tennessee came close to not ratifying the amendment that gave women the right to vote. The state legislators were divided almost evenly on the issue, but the side against ratification had one more supporter than did the pro-ratification side. At the last minute a young state senator named Harry Burn, who had seemed to be solidly against women voting, suddenly changed his  mind and supported his former opponents. The Nineteenth Amendment passed. When asked later why he had switched sides, Burn said that he had received a telegram from his mother asking him to support the right of women like her to have a voice in their government.

Another intense conflict has been the struggle for racial equality. In 1890 many of the rights blacks had won during the Civil War and Reconstruction era were taken away from them. The Ku Klux Klan was revived, and its members terrorized and killed blacks to prevent them from fighting for equal rights. Blacks suspected of offenses as insignificant as being rude to a white person were lynched—attacked by a mob and killed.

POPULATION GROWTH: 1790–2000

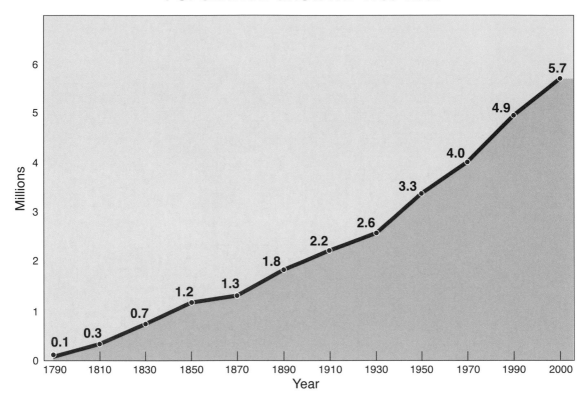

Their bodies were sometimes left hanging in public places to frighten others. Between 1880 and 1950 approximately two hundred black Tennesseans were lynched. New "Jim Crow" laws separated the races on buses, in schools, and even in parks.

In 1950 parents in the town of Clinton filed a lawsuit to force local authorities to allow African-American children to attend neighborhood schools rather than being bused to schools far from home. In 1954 the U.S. Supreme Court ordered school integration. By signing a paper called the Southern Manifesto, however, many southern senators defied this law.

African-American students arrive at Clinton High School on September 4, 1956, despite anti-integration demonstrations.

The Tennessee senator Estes Kefauver's refusal to sign it made him many enemies. School integration began in most of Tennessee in 1956, although Memphis did not integrate until 1961. Ellen Smith was a girl when the Nashville schools were integrated. "There were lots of demonstrations against integration downtown," she recalls. "People were furious. I remember worrying that our housekeeper wouldn't like us anymore because we were white. But she never mentioned the riots to me." For a while the process seemed to go smoothly, until three bombs destroyed much of the now-integrated Clinton High School. An elementary school in Nashville was bombed a year later. Students, especially in Nashville, organized sit-ins and other protests demanding an end to the violence and to segregation in schools, restaurants, public transportation, and stores.

The voting rights of African Americans were restored in the 1960s. It did not take long for them to start making their mark in Tennessee politics. In 1964 A. W. Willis Jr. became the first African American elected to the Tennessee legislature. It took more than thirty years before Tennessee had an African-American chief justice of the state supreme court, A. A. Birch Jr., in 1996.

The civil rights leader Dr. Martin Luther King Jr., who had won a Nobel Peace Prize for his nonviolent crusade for equal rights, went to Memphis in 1968 to try to help the city's sanitation workers, who were on strike. In one of the most tragic episodes of American history, King was assassinated there, and today a civil rights museum stands on the spot where he was killed.

Tennesseans have fought long and hard, sometimes against each other, to get where they are today. As President Theodore Roosevelt put it, "No state has a more remarkable and romantic history than Tennessee."

A. A. Birch Jr. is the first African-American man to hold the position of chief justice of the Tennessee Supreme Court.

Chapter Three

Woven from a
Single Thread

Who are Tennesseans? Where did their ancestors come from? Today, the traditional three-part division of the state holds less true about the people than about the geography. In the past, though, people were more tied to the land, so geographic differences led to different ways of life.

East Tennessee consisted mostly of small farms and tiny, isolated communities. This was due to the independent spirit of the people who lived there as well as to the difficulty of traveling in the hills in the days before interstate highways. And the hilly, rocky terrain of East Tennessee did not lend itself to the creation of large plantations, so the area had very few slaves.

Most settlers of Middle and West Tennessee, the flatter parts of the state, emigrated from Virginia and North Carolina. They brought slaves and the plantation system with them. Farms in Middle and West Tennessee thus tended to be bigger than those in East Tennessee. Great numbers of people,

Tennessee's population consists of a diverse group of people who contribute to the strong cultural mix of the state.

both enslaved and free, worked the land. In the west, cattle and horses grazed in the fields, while farmers in the east tended to raise hardier, smaller animals (such as pigs and goats) that could graze on the hillsides.

The emigrants from North Carolina and Virginia also brought many customs with them. Among these was laying out towns with a common town square or green and a community church. This, combined with the greater ease of travel in the Middle Tennessee hills and the West Tennessee flatlands, allowed for the growth of larger communities in these areas.

Although most people in the central and western parts of the state work in cities and towns today, the past still shapes people's lives. Carol Hamlett's great-great-great-grandfather moved from North Carolina to West Ten-nessee's Crockett County in 1843. His cotton farm prospered, and Carol grew up in the large house he had built. Her family still farmed cotton when she was a child, but by the 1950s a series of regulations limited the amount of cotton any one farm could produce, so they moved off the land.

Hamlett says, "Once the cotton allotment laws were passed, it was hard for people to make a living in West Tennessee. When you go there, it's like stepping back in time. This is part of the charm of the area, but it's also depressing—things haven't changed because people don't have the jobs and the money to make a change."

In Tennessee, newcomers formed communities, which grew to become towns.

ETHNIC TENNESSEE

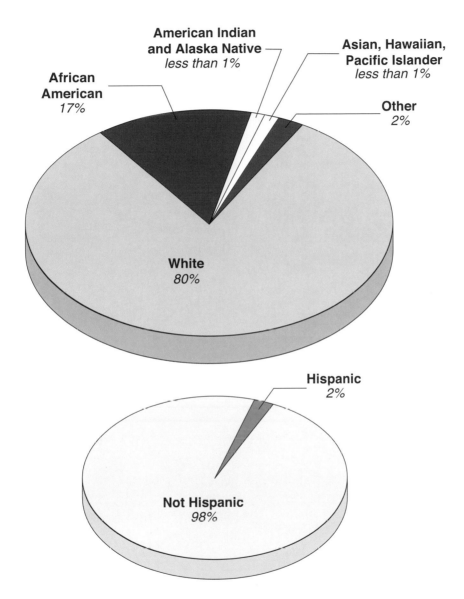

**American Indian
and Alaska Native**
less than 1%

**Asian, Hawaiian,
Pacific Islander**
less than 1%

**African
American**
17%

Other
2%

White
80%

Hispanic
2%

Not Hispanic
98%

*Note: A person of Cuban, Mexican, Puerto Rican, South or Central American,
or other Spanish culture or origin, regardless of race is defined as Hispanic.*

ETHNIC TENNESSEE

Almost all Tennesseans—99 percent—were born in the United States. The number of Tennesseans born in the state is also much higher than the national average. Now the numbers of immigrants are beginning to increase. In 2004 Tennessee's population of 5,748,379 comprised 4,600,100 white residents, 935,023 African Americans, 72,931 Asians, 14,718 Native American and Alaskan Natives, and 4,784 Native Hawaiian or other Pacific Islanders (some people identified themselves as belonging to more than one race). The Hispanic population, although growing, is still small. Recently, the state has seen an increasing number of Japanese immigrants. Meiji Gakuin High School in Sweetwater was the first fully accredited Japanese high school in the United States. These new Tennesseans have brought different religions, traditions, arts, foods, stories, and games to the state.

In general, more Tennessean African Americans live in cities than live in rural areas. Nashville's population is about 26 percent black, while Memphis is almost 61 percent black. The cities in general have shown a decline in the black population since the 1950s, when many African-American people migrated from the South to seek work in the cities of the North.

Tennessee's population is becoming more diverse, as can be seen from the student body population of Kirkpatrick Elementary School in Nashville.

POPULATION DENSITY

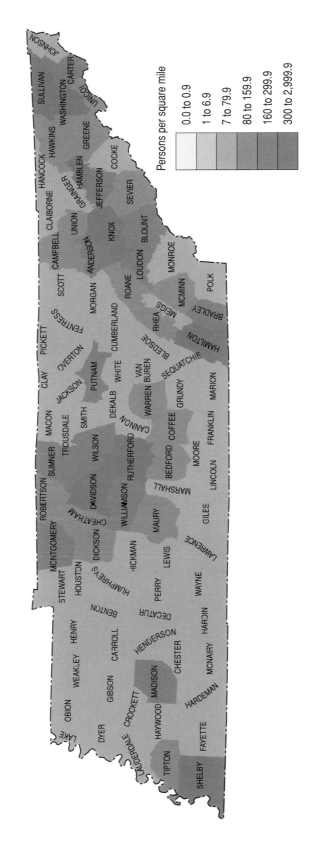

Persons per square mile

0.0 to 0.9	1 to 6.9	7 to 79.9	80 to 159.9	160 to 299.9	300 to 2,999.9

JOHNSON
SULLIVAN
CARTER
UNICOI
WASHINGTON
GREENE
HAWKINS
COCKE
HANCOCK
HAMBLEN
CLAIBORNE
GRAINGER
JEFFERSON
SEVIER
CAMPBELL
UNION
KNOX
BLOUNT
SCOTT
ANDERSON
LOUDON
MONROE
MORGAN
ROANE
MCMINN
POLK
FENTRESS
CUMBERLAND
RHEA
MEIGS
BRADLEY
PICKETT
WHITE
BLEDSOE
HAMILTON
CLAY
OVERTON
PUTNAM
VAN BUREN
SEQUATCHIE
JACKSON
DEKALB
WARREN
GRUNDY
MARION
MACON
SMITH
CANNON
COFFEE
FRANKLIN
TROUSDALE
WILSON
BEDFORD
MOORE
SUMNER
RUTHERFORD
LINCOLN
ROBERTSON
DAVIDSON
MARSHALL
GILES
MCNTGOMERY
CHEATHAM
WILLIAMSON
MAURY
DICKSON
LAWRENCE
STEWART
HICKMAN
LEWIS
HOUSTON
HUMPHREY'S
PERRY
WAYNE
BENTON
DECATUR
HARDIN
HENRY
HENDERSON
CHESTER
WEAKLEY
CARROLL
MCNAIRY
OBION
GIBSON
MADISON
HARDEMAN
DYER
CROCKETT
HAYWOOD
FAYETTE
LAKE
LAUDERDALE
TIPTON
SHELBY

"Before the arrival of the settlers," says Tennessean Allison Shaw, who is half Native American, "the Indians lived like kings and queens of the land." The rich religious and spiritual lives of the Cherokees and other tribes were a vital part of their cultures. Many of their traditional beliefs and practices were destroyed by the disruption of their way of life when the white settlers moved in. By the time of the Trail of Tears, almost all the Cherokees who lived in Tennessee had been Christian for two generations.

Today, some Native Americans are learning about their tribes' traditional religious beliefs and feel they can combine their Christian faith with a respect

Native Americans in traditional costume celebrate their culture and heritage at a powwow in Nashville.

for their ancestral ways. However, that can be difficult. Shaw was shocked by the stereotypes that some people held about Native Americans. One day, outside a movie theater where she had taken her two young children to see Disney's *Pocahontas*, another theatergoer said to her, "Everyone knows that Indians are devil worshipers." Shaw corrected the woman but felt stung that a fellow Christian would have so little regard and understanding for someone else's beliefs.

Because of the great number of Christian fundamentalist religions in the South, the area is sometimes called the Bible Belt. As the home of the 16-million-member Southern Baptist Convention, the largest group of Protestants in the United States, Tennessee is like the buckle on that belt. There are by far more Southern Baptists in Tennessee than followers of any other religion. Next come the Methodists, followed by Presbyterians and members of the Church of Christ.

One unusual form of Protestantism exists mostly in the Appalachian Mountains of Tennessee and Kentucky: snake handling. A passage in the Bible (Mark 16:18) says, "They shall take up serpents and if they drink any deadly thing, it shall in no way hurt them." Snake handlers believe this means anyone who truly believes in Jesus and lives a good life can pick up poisonous snakes and drink poison, but not be harmed.

To prove the depth of their faith, some believers handle snakes and drink small amounts of poison in their religious services. Worshipers are occasionally bitten, sometimes fatally. Snake handling was made illegal in 1973 because of worries that children were being harmed. Still, in parts of Tennessee, Kentucky, and Indiana, a few churches still practice it.

While the majority of Tennesseans are Protestants, the Catholic and Jewish populations are growing, especially in the larger cities. Many Asians in Middle Tennessee are bringing religions such as Buddhism to the area as well.

While most Tennesseans practice Protestantism, other religious sects are growing in the region.

When Eva Baker was a child in Nashville in the 1920s, everyone she knew was a Protestant. "It wasn't till I was in high school that I met my first Catholic," she says, "and it was a real shock to me!" Her son knew both Protestants and Catholics as a child but did not have a Jewish acquaintance until he was in high school in the 1960s. In Nashville in the 1990s, his children had Protestant, Catholic, Jewish, Buddhist, Hindu, Unitarian, Quaker, and atheist friends.

MELUNGEONS

An English explorer named Abraham Wood mentions in his 1673 journal that he found living on the Tennessee River "a white people which have long beardes and whiskers and weares clothing." The settlers said that these people, who called themselves Melungeons, spoke English and practiced Christianity. They were olive-skinned and tall, with black hair and eyes.

Melungeons still live in East Tennessee, mostly in the very isolated Hancock County. There are several theories about their origin. Some believe they are the descendants of the first English settlers at Roanoke, Virginia, who mysteriously disappeared in the sixteenth century. Others say they could be descendants of white explorers and escaped slaves who married Native Americans.

The Melungeons themselves say they are descended from Portuguese explorers. Since Melungeons suffer from diseases common to people from Mediterranean countries such as Portugal, their claim is likely to be true.

Nowhere is the division between the regions of Tennessee more obvious than in the history of race relations. Before the Civil War slavery was more prevalent in the middle and western parts of the state than in the east, mostly because of the differences in ways of farming.

Carol Hamlett's ancestor Asa Robertson owned twenty-three slaves in West Tennessee in the 1850s. When her great-grandparents gave some land to Crockett County in the 1940s for the purpose of building a school, they made it clear that the school was to be for white children only. Hamlett says, "When my mother moved down there from New York State in 1945, she was shocked to see that there were still slave cabins on the property."

Blacks, most of them slaves, were taken to Tennessee with the earliest settlers. Until the Civil War both enslaved and free blacks in the state worked mostly on farms, with a smaller number working in iron foundries or as house servants. When their freedom was granted, few had the education or experience necessary to get highly skilled jobs. It was a difficult fight for them to achieve some measure of equality.

Integration was slow, and conflicts were frequent. A major race riot erupted in the Middle Tennessee town of Columbia in 1946 following a fistfight between a black man and a white man.

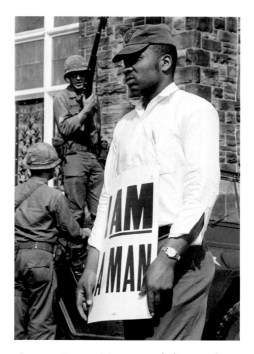

Integration in Tennessee did not take hold quickly. This 1968 demonstrator in Memphis wore a placard reading, "I AM A MAN."

After four days of violence, two black men were dead, dozens had been beaten, and Columbia's entire black district was destroyed.

Even so, little by little, Tennesseans of different races began living together in relative harmony. The small towns of East Tennessee had included both black and white congregation members in most of their churches. During the nineteenth century, a time when blacks and whites were not even buried in the same graveyards, people of both races were interred at the City Cemetery of Nashville, making it one of the oldest integrated cemeteries in the country.

Race relations are far from perfect in Tennessee. Yet Stacy Franklin, who moved to Nashville in 1989, feels far more at ease living there than she did in the North. Stacy, who is African American, and Jack, her white husband, were frightened by racist taunting in the northern city in which they both grew up. Stacy's sister moved to Nashville, and she advised Stacy, "Move down here—no one cares about mixed-race couples in Nashville." Stacy and Jack did just that and are happily raising their children in Nashville. "I feel more comfortable here than anyplace else," said Stacy.

Jill Martin disagrees. Martin, who is white, stopped attending her church after a member of the congregation told her that her daughter's birth defect was God's punishment for her marrying an African-American man. "I know she's not the only one who thinks that way," said Martin, still furious over the incident, which took place ten years ago. "I know I should forgive her, but God hasn't softened my heart that much yet."

Relations between Native Americans and people of European ancestry in Tennessee are improving, according to Allison Shaw: "There's less prejudice here than in states where Indians live on reservations. Tennessee has always been a state that prides itself on valuing families and communities, and these have always been important to Indian people, too.

Organizations, such as the Alliance for Native American Indian Rights in Nashville, dedicate themselves to the protection and preservation of native culture.

There's very little discrimination in jobs and housing against native peoples." She adds that the solidarity in the Native American community gives all of them strength: "Being Indian is like being part of this huge tapestry that has lots of colors and patterns and textures, but it's all woven from a single thread, and that thread runs through all of us. There are differences in culture, in language, in spiritual belief, but we are all tied together."

FRIED CORN

Almost all the people who formed early communities in Tennessee counted on the fertile land to provide them with food. The inexperienced settlers of Rugby were so confident that they could earn money selling their surplus produce that they printed up labels for the cans they were going to use. One of them shows a large lady in long skirts on top of a ladder, cheerfully plucking tomatoes off a tree! Perhaps the labels were never used because the Rugbians discovered tomatoes actually grow on vines that flourish low to the ground.

The best recipes from Tennessee rely on what thrives there, especially fresh produce and hogs.

Have an adult help you cut the kernels off five ears of very fresh corn, preferably white corn. With a spoon, scrape the cobs to get out the small bits of corn that remain.

Melt 2 tablespoons of bacon grease in a large skillet. Add the corn, 1/2 teaspoon salt, a pinch of pepper, a pinch of sugar, and 1/4 cup water. Cook over low heat, stirring occasionally, until corn is tender (about 10 minutes). Add a little more water if the corn starts to stick. Serve hot with ham and biscuits.

Chapter Four

Beyond Watauga

In 1772 a band of settlers in East Tennessee organized themselves into a group called the Watauga Association. They were led by James Robertson and John Sevier, who later became Tennessee's first governor. The members of the Watauga Association wrote the Articles, the first written constitution in America. Some think it was based at least in part on the laws of the Iroquois Federation.

Since many of Tennessee's settlers had gone to the new territory to escape the colonial government, they resented this new control. Most of these independent-minded people settled in the remote eastern hills, far from government of any kind. Today, the residents of East Tennessee still have a reputation for disliking government and preferring to settle their problems among themselves, without what they call "interference" from the authorities.

But most Tennesseans recognize the need for a state government. Tennessee's first constitution was approved when the territory became a state in 1796. A new one was approved in 1834, and a third in 1870. This latter document, with several amendments, is the one in force in Tennessee today.

Modeled after a Greek Ionic temple, Tennessee's capitol building houses the governor's offices, the Senate, House of Representatives, and constitutional offices.

Like the nation itself and most states, Tennessee has three branches of government: the legislative, the executive, and the judicial.

Legislative

Tennessee's legislative branch is responsible for making the laws for the state. The legislature, called the General Assembly, contains two bodies: the senate, with thirty-three members, and the house of representatives, with ninety-nine. The members of the General Assembly are elected by the communities they live in and represent.

Two presidents of the United States, James K. Polk and Andrew Jackson, began their careers as Tennessee state legislators. Davy Crockett, the nineteenth-century frontiersman who later became a U.S. congressman and then died at the Alamo in Texas, was a Tennessee legislator, as was Cordell Hull, the longest-serving United States secretary of state.

Executive

The executive branch of Tennessee's government is headed by the governor. Most governors have been Democrats— since 1881, there have been only six Republican governors of Tennessee. The governor recommends new laws to the General Assembly. If the assembly passes a law that the governor does not approve of, he (all of Tennessee's governors have been men) may veto, or cancel, it.

James K. Polk served in the Tennessee legislature before becoming governor of Tennessee and later as president of the United States.

Tennessee governor Phil Bredesen visits with students in a pre-K class at Fall-Hamilton Elementary School in Nashville.

The governor is the head of the state militia (army). He also appoints the judges and the commissioners who head the various departments.

Judicial

The state courts and the judges who preside over them make up the judicial branch of the government. There are four levels of courts. The highest is the state supreme court. Below it are the intermediate appellate courts, then the four courts (probate, criminal, circuit, and chancery) that make up the trial courts. At the lowest level are the courts of limited jurisdiction, such as the juvenile courts.

In some counties the judges are elected by the people. In others they are appointed by the mayor. The kinds of cases the different courts rule on also vary from county to county. Some crimes are covered by more than one court, making it difficult to decide who should conduct the trial. Sometimes it takes an expert lawyer just to figure out which court should hear a particular case. Tennessee is unusual in having a chancery court, in which cases are tried when the exact meaning of a law is unclear. Few states in the country still have chancery courts.

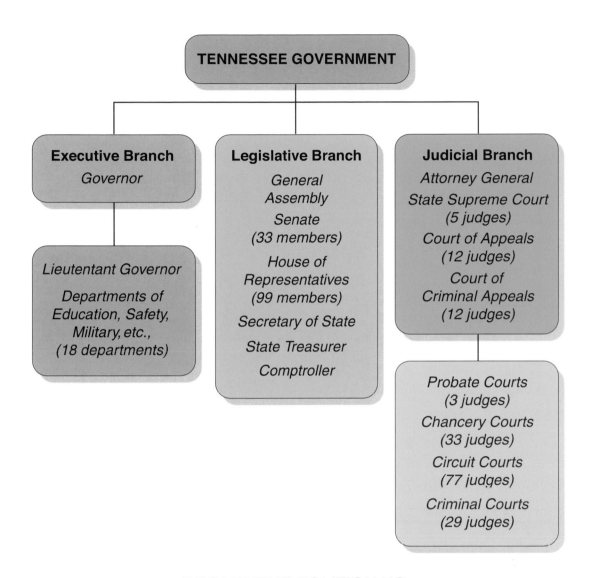

TENNESSEE GOVERNMENT

Executive Branch
Governor

Lieutentant Governor

Departments of Education, Safety, Military, etc., (18 departments)

Legislative Branch
General Assembly

Senate (33 members)

House of Representatives (99 members)

Secretary of State

State Treasurer

Comptroller

Judicial Branch
Attorney General

State Supreme Court (5 judges)

Court of Appeals (12 judges)

Court of Criminal Appeals (12 judges)

Probate Courts (3 judges)

Chancery Courts (33 judges)

Circuit Courts (77 judges)

Criminal Courts (29 judges)

PROMINENT POLITICIANS

Many Tennesseans have served with distinction in the federal government, three of them as president: Andrew Jackson (1829–1837), James K. Polk (1845–1849), and Andrew Johnson (1865–1869).

Andrew Jackson was the first American president from west of the Appalachians. All earlier presidents were from wealthy families, but Jackson was born in a log cabin and grew up on the frontier. His father died a few days before he was born, and he lost his mother when he was fourteen. Jackson fought at least two duels, killing his opponent in one of them. His toughness earned him the nickname Old Hickory. A famous soldier, Jackson was very popular during his presidency, especially with people in the western United States.

In the 1840s Tennessee grew in both size and importance. Governor James K. Polk was elected president in 1844, even though his own state did not vote for him. The Mexican War was fought during Polk's presidency. His fellow Tennesseans rallied to support their president, and 25,000 of them volunteered for military service.

Tennessee senator Andrew Johnson had remained loyal to the Union before and during the Civil War and was the only Southern senator to speak up against secession. He was elected vice president in 1864 and became president in 1865, when Lincoln was assassinated. The Northerners thought he, a Southerner, was being too easy on the South. Southerners, on the other hand, could not forgive his siding with the Union. He was impeached (brought to trial) in 1868 and was acquitted by just one vote.

For Tennessee, Andrew Johnson served as a senator and as governor before becoming president in 1865.

Cordell Hull served as U.S. secretary of state during World War II and became one of the organizers of the United Nations. He won the Nobel Peace Prize in 1945.

Senator Howard Baker, from Huntsville, Tennessee, was the Senate minority leader and then majority leader during much of the 1970s and 1980s. He was one of the leaders of the committee that investigated the Watergate scandal when President Richard Nixon was suspected of committing crimes in his effort to be reelected president. Baker also served as President Ronald Reagan's chief of staff.

Lamar Alexander was Tennessee's governor from 1978 to 1987. He then served as the secretary of education under President George Bush. He ran unsuccessfully for the Republican presidential nomination in 1996.

Tennesseans continue to be well represented in the U.S. government. The former Tennessee senator Al Gore served as vice president under Bill Clinton (1993–2001) and in 2000 narrowly missed being elected president of the United States. Senator Bill Frist was elected U.S. Senate majority leader in 2003.

Not all of Tennessee's politicians have behaved honorably. Governor Ray Blanton (1975–1979) spent his last days in office pardoning convicted criminals in exchange for payment. The inauguration of his successor was moved up three days to force an end to this practice. In 2005 four state legislators were charged with accepting bribes to help get laws passed that would help private companies.

Al Gore, vice president of the United States 1993–2001

TENNESSEE
BY COUNTY

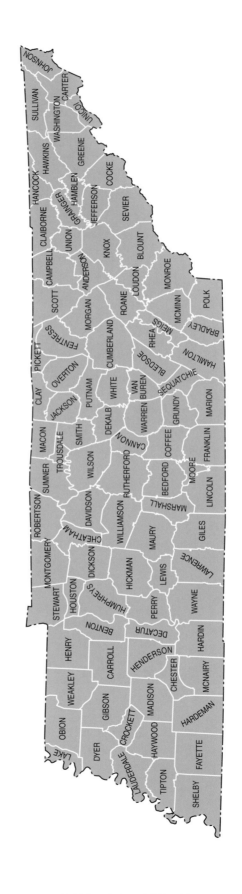

THE MONKEY TRIAL

One of the most famous legal battles in American history, the Scopes "Monkey Trial," took place in Dayton, Tennessee, in 1925. Tennessee had outlawed the teaching of evolution, making it illegal for any teacher to "teach any theory that denies the story of the Divine Creation of man as taught in the Bible, and to teach instead that man has descended from a lower order of animals." A teacher named John Thomas Scopes thought that this law was wrong and deliberately broke it to force a court to hear the case. Scopes lost his case. Evolution was not legally taught in Tennessee until 1967.

History almost repeated itself in 1995 when the Tennessee legislature tried to pass a new law requiring evolution to be taught as scientific theory, not fact. The bill was defeated.

Tennessee's governor Phil Bredesen, who was formerly the mayor of Nashville, is an important member of the Democratic Party. Many people think he will run for president one day. Whether or not he does, Tennesseeans will continue to play an important part in the governing of the United States.

Chapter Five

Economic Strides

Whether it's due to good management or to other factors, Tennesseans' lives are getting better in many ways. Exports are growing, as is the state's economy as a whole. The employment rate is now higher than the national average.

The first factories in Tennessee were built in the 1880s. They were mostly textile mills. Manufacturing boomed in the state in the 1950s and 1960s. Today, manufacturing accounts for 22 percent of the state's economy and employs almost half a million Tennesseans. Chemicals, transportation equipment, rubber, and plastics are the most important industries.

The automobile industry is also growing. Before World War I a car called the Marathon was made in Tennessee, but it never became popular, and the factory shut down after a few years. Car manufacturing returned to the state in 1982 when Nissan opened a plant in Smyrna. Today, it is the largest single automobile factory in the United States. General Motors' Saturn plant in Spring Hill also employs many people. In 2005 the Nissan corporation announced the relocation of its North

Tennessee's industrial sector has enjoyed much success, accounting for more than 20 percent of the state's income.

A Saturn vehicle is assembled at the Spring Hill plant.

American headquarters to the Nashville area. Tennessee is now the fifth-largest auto-manufacturing state in the nation.

Farming has declined as a source of income in Tennessee since the nineteenth century, but it is still important, especially in the middle and western parts of the state. Soybeans, tobacco, cotton, wheat, and corn are the most important crops. Unfortunately, much of the land was overfarmed in the past, and fewer acres are being devoted to farming today.

In the first half of the twentieth century, people fled the poorly producing farms and moved to the cities. By 1960 more Tennesseans lived in cities than in the country. Many of them worked in the factories that sprang up all over the state. Between 1955 and 1965 Tennessee's industries grew faster than those of any other state, and in 1963 Tennessee ranked sixteenth in the nation for industrial output.

A farmer checks the quality and growth of his tobacco crop.

2003 GROSS STATE PRODUCT: $203 Million

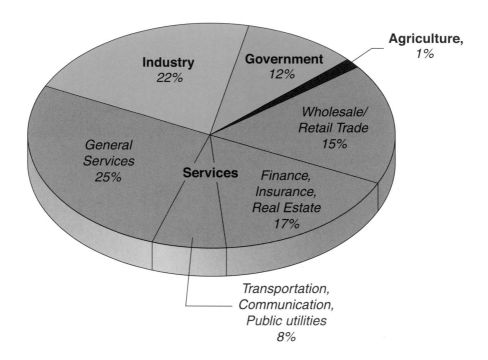

Industry
22%

Government
12%

Agriculture,
1%

Wholesale/
Retail Trade
15%

General
Services
25%

Services

Finance,
Insurance,
Real Estate
17%

Transportation,
Communication,
Public utilities
8%

THE TENNESSEE VALLEY AUTHORITY

Tennesseans are in general poorer than most other Americans. In 2002 Tennessee ranked twenty-eighth out of the fifty states in the average income of its residents. This is an improvement over 1998, when it was in thirty-third place. And in 1996 Tennessee led the nation in job and income gains.

These gains represent a vast improvement since 1929, the first year of the Great Depression, which plunged much of the country into unemployment and poverty. The Depression hit Tennessee hard. The whole country suffered, but the Southeast was worse off than other regions: the average income of a Tennessean in 1929 was only about half the national average.

During the Depression many families in Tennessee suffered. This family sometimes earned only $19 per month.

To help the state and the region, the federal government started a program called the Tennessee Valley Authority (TVA) in 1933. The TVA built dams on the Tennessee River and its tributaries. These dams brought electricity to parts of Tennessee for the first time. They also controlled floods and created lakes. Some Tennesseans were opposed to the construction of dams, especially when their homes were to be flooded by the resulting lakes. Although they were paid for their property, some had to be forcibly removed by federal agents.

The Norris Dam was one of the first dams built by the Tennessee Valley Authority. It can generate about 131,400 kilowatts of electricity.

EARNING A LIVING

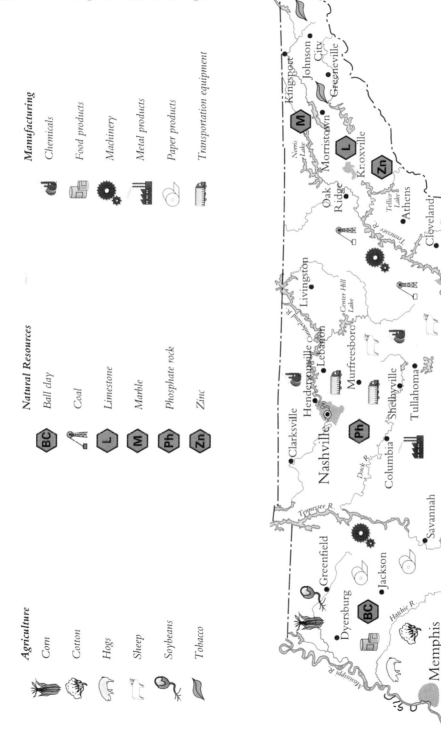

Agriculture

- Corn
- Cotton
- Hogs
- Sheep
- Soybeans
- Tobacco

Natural Resources

- **BC** Ball clay
- Coal
- **L** Limestone
- **M** Marble
- **Ph** Phosphate rock
- **Zn** Zinc

Manufacturing

- Chemicals
- Food products
- Machinery
- Metal products
- Paper products
- Transportation equipment

Other federal programs, such as the Civilian Conservation Corps (CCC), employed out-of-work Tennesseans in construction projects. "They did a lot of things for the people in the state," said Greg Giles. "The park shelters built by the CCC are wonderful. But you have to have mixed feelings about the TVA. A lot of people in Tennessee might still be without electricity if the TVA hadn't come in, but they disrupted a lot of people's lives by flooding their homes."

During the 1940s, the TVA employed more than 25,000 people.

EDUCATION

Lack of education among Tennesseans has hurt the state's economy. The nineteenth-century philanthropist George Peabody, a northerner, gave the state money to support its public schools. Even so, in 1900 fewer than half of Tennessee's children attended school. Although that number has increased dramatically, in 2002 Tennessee had one of the lowest graduation rates in the nation with only 57 percent of its students graduating from high school.

To improve student performance, Tennessee is expected to provide better teacher training and at least ninety minutes of reading instruction each day.

Teachers' salaries are below the national average, and the state ranks last or close to last in the amount of money it spends on public education.

School integration was resisted in much of the state until the federal government stepped in. Today, Nashville is considered by some to be a national model of school integration, although some residents, both black and white, think the money spent on busing students to schools in different neighborhoods should be put directly into the schools themselves. Education in the state continues to improve, with about half of every tax dollar going to fund public schools. In 1996 Tennessee became the first state in the nation to have every public school linked to the Internet.

Tennessee imposed a tax on tobacco in 1925 to help fund its public schools. This tax has been an important source of funding for education.

Tennessee lottery president Rebecca Paul celebrates the lottery's first year of sales with $246 million earmarked for education.

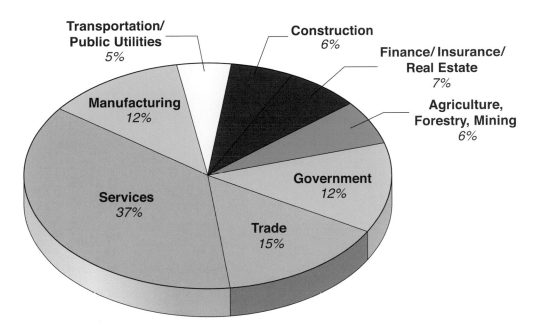

TENNESSEE WORKFORCE

Transportation/
Public Utilities
5%

Construction
6%

Finance/Insurance/
Real Estate
7%

Agriculture,
Forestry, Mining
6%

Manufacturing
12%

Government
12%

Services
37%

Trade
15%

But as people smoke less, the state's funding for education has dropped. In order to make up this loss, Tennessee passed a law allowing a state lottery in 2002. Proceeds from the sales of lottery tickets are set aside to provide scholarships for Tennessee residents to attend state colleges and universities and to make improvements to school buildings and provide after-school programs.

Great strides have been made in improving the economy of Tennessee. But the state's residents still disagree over the best way to attract new business. Some want to weaken the already feeble environmental laws to make it less expensive for manufacturers to operate in Tennessee. Others argue that the state's natural beauty is one of its most precious assets and will by itself draw new businesses into the area.

Some say that spending money on education will make Tennesseans more productive workers and will encourage more people to move to the state, while others say that tax money would be better spent on building factories and giving tax breaks to new businesses.

Today, nearly 22 percent of the state's income comes from manufacturing. Tourism continues to be important, as lovers of country music, beautiful parks, and other attractions travel to Tennessee. The state is trying to get visitors to discover other aspects of Tennessee. As part of an effort to make the state a better-known vacation destination, Nashville mayor (and later Tennessee governor) Phil Bredesen spearheaded the construction of a huge sports stadium, the Coliseum, in the city. The Houston Oilers football team moved there in 1997 and were later renamed the Tennessee Titans.

In 2004, Tennessee earned over $10 billion in tourist dollars. It is the eleventh most-visited state in the United States.

New funding is also coming from a traditional source: tobacco. But it's not the sale of the plant that is bringing in the dollars this time. Instead, in 1998 Tennessee and other states reached an agreement with major cigarette manufacturers to be reimbursed for health-care expenses incurred because of tobacco use. Every year until at least 2025, Tennessee will receive up to $4.8 billion from this agreement.

In the Growers Settlement Trust, cigarette manufacturers compensate Tennessee tobacco growers billions of dollars each year for lost income if the demand for tobacco declines.

Chapter Six

Exploring Tennessee

Tennessee is very popular with vacationers. Great Smoky Mountain National Park, in East Tennessee and North Carolina, is the most popular of all national parks in the United States, hosting some 9 million visitors every year. More tour buses go to Nashville than to any other city in the country. Millions of people visit Graceland, Elvis Presley's Memphis home. Visitors can find spectacular scenery, charming small towns, and lively festivals all across the state.

Tennessee's beautiful scenery draws sportspeople as well. The world's largest artificial ski surface is located in Gatlinburg in the Smokies. People travel from all over the world to explore Tennessee's caves and mountains. So exciting are the state's white-water rapids that the 1996 Summer Olympics, held in Atlanta, moved to Tennessee's Ocoee River for the white-water events.

THE MOUNTAINOUS EAST

Great Smoky Mountain National Park is the major attraction in East Tennessee. The Cherokee called the area the Land of a Thousand Smokes

A visit to Tennessee wouldn't be complete without a tour of the Great Smoky Mountain National Park.

Great Smoky Mountain National Park offers more than eight hundred miles of trails to hike and hosts more than 3,500 plant species.

because of the haze that hangs over the mountains. Today, the more than 500,000-acre park is home to many birds, mammals, and plants. You can find twenty-six species of salamander—more than in any other area of the same size. Unfortunately, in 2000 the National Parks Conservation Association named this park one of the ten most endangered national parks in the United States.

Gatlinburg is the town nearest the park. Its population of less than four thousand is overwhelmed by the millions of visitors who pass through each year. Crammed with motels and souvenir shops, Gatlinburg exists for the tourist trade.

About five miles away is Pigeon Forge, where Dolly Parton's theme park, Dollywood, houses crafts shops and other attractions. The big draw, though, is country music.

Knoxville is the largest city in the eastern portion of the state. It has come a long way since the author John Gunther wrote in 1946, "Knoxville is the ugliest city I ever saw in America [and] is one of the least orderly cities in the South." Home to the largest campus of the University of Tennessee, Knoxville hosted the 1982 World's Fair. The three-hundred-foot-tall tower of the Sunsphere still stands at the site of the fair.

The Knoxville Museum of Art, housed near the Eleventh Street Artists' Colony of art galleries and studios, offers music and lectures as well as works or art. Every April the city's Dogwood Arts Festival attracts visitors, who can walk six different dogwood trails and attend many different crafts fairs and concerts.

The World's Fair Park in Nashville includes lawns, gardens, waterfalls, and streams that create the perfect setting for festivals, meetings, and leisure activities.

PLACES TO SEE

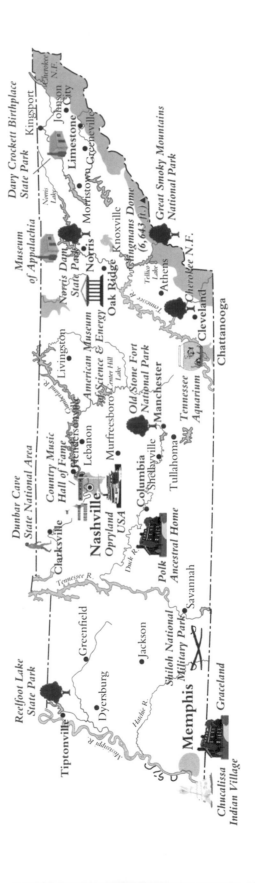

Also in East Tennessee is Oak Ridge, where the developers of the atom bomb worked in secrecy during World War II. The American Museum of Science and Energy, developed by the United States Department of Energy, is one of the world's largest museums devoted to this topic.

Jonesborough hosts the National Storytelling Festival in October. This festival grows each year, as storytellers from all over the United States and around the world come to learn more about their art, to hear other tellers' stories, and to enter competitions.

PLATEAU AND VALLEY REGION

Chattanooga is home to Lookout Mountain. The Cherokee name for this towering cliff is Chatunuga, which means "the rock which comes to an end." There you will find the Incline Railway, perhaps the world's steepest passenger railroad. The mountain is so tall that on a good day, a visitor can see seven states from its peak. An important Civil War conflict, called the Battle Above the Clouds, was fought on Lookout Mountain in 1863, and nearby is the largest and oldest military park in the United States: Chickamauga and Chattanooga National Military Park.

Visitors view several states from Lookout Mountain.

The natural wonders outside Chattanooga also attract many visitors. Nearby is Ruby Falls, which at 145 feet is the highest underground waterfall in the United States. The falls are 1,120 feet below the ground. Rock City, a park with caves, rock formations, and oddly shaped boulders, is a popular spot for tourists.

Ruby Falls was discovered by Leo Lambert in the late 1920s. He named the falls after his wife, Ruby.

Chattanooga is home to the Tennessee Aquarium, which opened in 1992. This is the first large freshwater-fish aquarium in the world. Visitors take an elevator to the top of the museum, then walk down the spiraling ramp, following the course of a stream from the Smoky Mountains to the Gulf of Mexico. Along the way natural habitats are recreated that house seven thousand animals, including three hundred species of fish, birds, reptiles, and amphibians.

Cumberland Mountain State Rustic Park, near Crossville, was built during the Great Depression by members of the Civilian Conservation Corps, local men who learned to perform construction work while creating cabins and clearings for others to enjoy. The cabins in the park are built mainly of local crab orchard stone, a honey-colored rock that abounds in the hills. The park also has campgrounds, a lake, and nature trails. Nearby is Fall Creek Falls State Park, which boasts a 256-foot waterfall, the highest east of the Rockies.

One of the most popular attractions in Tennessee is Fall Creek Falls State Park.

Nashville may be the state capital, but it is the country music that draws crowds of visitors each year. Not all Nashvilleans love this popular American music, however.

Nashville's nickname "Music City, U.S.A." usually makes people think of country music. It was a different kind of music, though, that inspired this name: the traditional African-American spirituals sung by the Fisk Jubilee Singers of Fisk University. This choral group toured the country and the world raising funds for building at their school. Fisk Jubilee Hall was built with the proceeds. Today, all kinds of music, from classical to rock, from pop to bluegrass (as well as country, of course!) can be heard in the city.

Nashville, named after Revolutionary War hero General Francis Nash, has been the state capital since 1843.

The centerpiece of Nashville's Centennial Park and symbol of the city is the Parthenon. An art museum can also be found in the Parthenon.

Middle Tennessee is an area rich in history. Nashville has been the capital since 1843. The capitol building was completed in 1859, making it one of the oldest state capitols in the country.

When Tennessee celebrated its one hundredth birthday in 1896, Nashville was still known as the "Athens of the South" because of all the universities there. One of the most popular exhibits in the Centennial Exposition was a full-sized wood-and-plaster copy of the Parthenon, the most famous monument of ancient Athens. When the original building disintegrated, it was rebuilt in concrete in Centennial Park, and today it is the symbol of the city. It is the only full-scale replica in the world that reproduces both the interior and exterior of the Greek temple. The forty-two-foot-tall statue of Athena inside the Nashville Parthenon is the largest indoor sculpture in the Western Hemisphere.

Nashville and its surrounding areas have many attractions for people interested in history. The Tennessee State Museum in downtown Nashville has exhibits on the history of the state, beginning with prehistoric times. Fort Nashborough, on the banks of the Cumberland River, is a replica of the original fort built by the settlers. The Frist Center for the Visual Arts opened in the former home of Nashville's main post office in 2001. Visitors can admire not only the art collected from around the world but also the magnificent old building.

The elegant 30,000-square-foot Cheekwood Mansion was once the private residence of the Cheek family. Today it is the centerpiece of the fifty-five-acre Cheekwood Botanical Garden and Museum of Art, open to the public since 1960. The mansion houses a permanent collection of art and also showcases many traveling art exhibits. The gardens and greenhouses, including a tranquil Japanese garden, an area devoted to native wildflowers, and other special plantings, are visited by about 190,000 people every year.

In Smyrna, outside Nashville, a visitor can tour the home of Sam Davis, known as the "Boy Hero of the Confederacy." Tour guides dressed in nineteenth-century costume lead visitors through the house and grounds, telling Sam Davis's story and showing what life on a prosperous farm of the time was like. Every May the grounds come alive for Sam Davis Days, as blacksmiths, weavers, soap makers, candle dippers, whittlers, and other craftspeople demonstrate the kinds of work the Davis family and their slaves would have done every day.

The Hermitage, Andrew Jackson's home, is also open to the public. Like Sam Davis's home, Jackson's gracious white house is furnished with nineteenth-century furniture.

Still, the big draw for most tourists in Middle Tennessee is country music. Nashville's six-block Music Row includes many souvenir shops.

The historic Ryman Auditorium, originally constructed as a religious revival house, was the original home of the *Grand Ole Opry*. The Opry now broadcasts from Gaylord Opryland Resort, on the eastern border of the city. The Opryland Hotel, a major convention center, is also located there. It is the seventh-largest hotel in the world (the top six are in Las Vegas).

Nashville is also home to two museums for children. The Nashville Toy Museum has exhibits of toys from centuries ago through the present. The Adventure Science Center hosts traveling scientific shows and has a planetarium as well as many permanent exhibits. Most of these are interactive, allowing visitors to find out firsthand the scientific principles involved in them.

Most of Nashville's festivals celebrate music. Summer Lights, held downtown every June, attracts bands of every kind to its large outdoor stages. The International Country Music Fan Fair, also in June, gives fans from around the world a chance to meet their favorite stars. This popular event frequently sells out all of its tickets before the show begins.

The Ryman Auditorium, built in 1892, was the concert hall where every country music star wanted to perform.

The Tennessee walking horse, famous for its unusually fast and smooth walk, comes from Middle Tennessee. Every year since 1939, the town of Shelbyville has hosted the Tennessee Walking Horse Celebration, during which these animals are shown and judged. Horses are also bought and sold at the celebration, along with all sorts of riding gear and souvenirs. Nearly a quarter of a million tickets are sold each year, and two thousand horses compete.

Farther south, near Manchester, is the mysterious Old Stone Fort. This huge structure, which includes a moat, was built by Native Americans before the arrival of the settlers, but when and for what purpose is unknown. Anthropologists believe that the area of about fifty acres on top of a hill was used as a central ceremonial gathering place for at least five hundred years.

TEN LARGEST CITIES

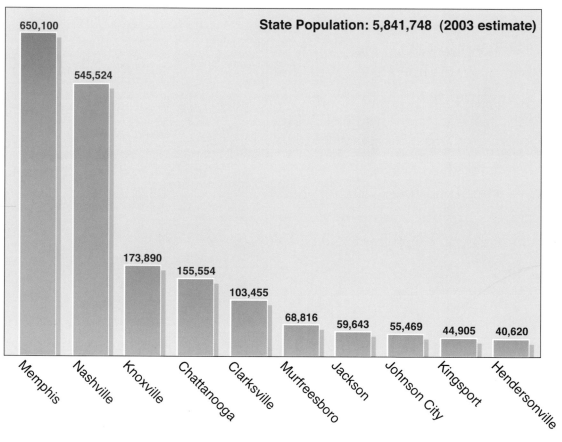

State Population: 5,841,748 (2003 estimate)

Memphis	650,100
Nashville	545,524
Knoxville	173,890
Chattanooga	155,554
Clarksville	103,455
Murfreesboro	68,816
Jackson	59,643
Johnson City	55,469
Kingsport	44,905
Hendersonville	40,620

"IF IT AIN'T COUNTRY, IT AIN'T MUSIC"

There are more country-music radio stations in the United States than any other kind. This popular form of American music has its roots in the folk music of England, Ireland, and Scotland. It was brought to America during the seventeenth through the nineteenth centuries and was adapted by the people living in the Southeast.

As interest in this music grew, George D. Hay, a Memphis-born radio announcer, started a new show called *National Barn Dance* on a Chicago radio station in the 1920s. He moved the show to Nashville in 1925 and began broadcasting *Barn Dance* on the radio station WSM.

Although the name of the program was soon changed to *The Grand Ole Opry*, the stage set still features a farm setting with a large barn in the middle. In 1943 the Opry moved to the 3,300-seat Ryman Auditorium in Nashville. The program was televised seven years later. By 1974 the Opry had outgrown Ryman Auditorium and moved to the Opryland USA Theme Park in East Nashville. The Opry theater remained open when the theme park closed and is now the world's largest broadcast studio. The Ryman Auditorium underwent major renovations costing $8.5 million and reopened as a theater hosting major music and dramatic performances.

The major attraction in West Tennessee is Memphis, with Elvis Presley's home, Graceland. Preserved as a shrine to the "King," as Presley is known, Graceland is the second-most-visited home in the United States (after the White House). People come to see where Presley lived with his wife and daughter and to admire the many sequined costumes worn by the performer. His tomb is often covered with flowers left by fans.

Memphis houses more than just Graceland, though. Music lovers flock to Beale Street, where the purely American form of music known as the blues was born. Concerts and performances, both indoor and outdoor, showcase traditional and modern forms of the blues.

Now a tourist haven, Graceland was the home of Elvis Presley from 1957 until his death in 1977.

Memphis' famous Beale Street is the perfect place to enjoy great music and entertainment.

The Chucalissa Museum shows what life in a Native American town was like before the coming of the settlers. It is located on the site of a town that existed for about seven centuries. Archaeologists have been excavating there, and several houses and a temple have been reconstructed.

Mud Island, in the middle of the Mississippi River, is home to several attractions, including an amphitheater and a theme park. The River Walk is a small-scale reproduction of the entire course of the Mississippi. The Mississippi River Museum has exhibits on the history and ecology of the longest river in North America.

Memphis, Egypt, is located next to the longest river on the continent of Africa, so Memphis, Tennessee, was named for the ancient Egyptian city. To celebrate the "sisterhood" of the two cities, the Tennessee city built a thirty-two-story, stainless steel pyramid on the banks of the Mississippi River. The structure is the third-largest pyramid in the world. It opened to the public in 1991 and hosted basketball games and art exhibits.

The Lorraine Motel, where Martin Luther King Jr. was assassinated, has been turned into the National Civil Rights Museum. The struggle of African Americans to achieve equal rights is chronicled there, with special attention given to King's Nobel Peace Prize-winning work.

One of the most popular attractions in Memphis is the twice-daily duck parade at the Peabody Hotel. Every morning a line of ducks waddles out to the lobby. Then they walk solemnly up velvet-covered steps to the fountain, where they swim all day. The performance is repeated in reverse in the evening, when the ducks strut down the steps and back to the elevator, then to the pen in their luxury penthouse to spend the night.

The 20,000-seat Pyramid Arena sits by the Mississippi River. No longer hosting sporting events, the arena houses traveling art exhibits and may have other uses in the future.

In Tennessee music and art, history and heritage, sports and recreation, and nature and wildlife are right at your doorstep.

Memphis holds a month-long festival called Memphis in May that celebrates a different country each year. Food, music, art, and performances from that country turn the city into a big party every evening and weekend in May. One of the highlights is the World Championship Barbecue Festival, during which visitors can sample dishes made not only with traditional pork, beef, and chicken but also with rattlesnake and ostrich!

In upper West Tennessee is 15,000-acre Reelfoot Lake. Its tranquil beauty and rich wildlife attract not only people who are interested in fishing but also naturalists who find a high concentration of bald eagles and other birds there. Eagle watch tours start in January and continue through March, the months when these magnificent birds fly through on their migratory route. "When I went to Reelfoot to see the bald eagles," remembers Sam Turner, "I thought, Big deal, they're just a big bird. But then when one swooped down, caught a fish, and then perched on a branch eating it, glaring at the people with one big eye, I realized it was truly awesome. We all stopped talking and looked at it as long as it sat on its branch. What a majestic creature!"

Majestic creatures, a romantic history, lofty mountains, fertile plains, friendly people—no wonder Tennesseans are proud of their state. People lucky enough to call Tennessee home are reluctant to move away, and newcomers quickly feel welcome and put down their own roots. Explore Tennessee and see its majesty for yourself!

THE FLAG: *The state flag of Tennessee has three white stars in a blue circle with a white ring around it. The three stars stand for the three "grand divisions" of Tennessee—East, Middle, and West. A thin white line at the right side of the flag separates the red background from a blue band. The flag was adopted in 1905.*

THE SEAL: *On the state seal a plow, wheat, and a cotton plant stand for agriculture in Tennessee. A riverboat represents commerce, or trade, in the state. The date 1796 is the year Tennessee became a state and approved its first constitution. The Roman number for 16 (XVI), at the top of the seal, shows that Tennessee is the sixteenth state to join the nation. The seal was first used during the term of Governor William G. Brownlow, who served from 1865 to 1869.*

State Survey

Statehood: June 1, 1796

Origin of Name: The name probably comes from "Tanasie," a Cherokee village in the area.

Nickname: Volunteer State or Big Bend State

Capital: Nashville

Motto: Agriculture and Commerce

Bird: Mockingbird

Flower: Iris

Tree: Tulip poplar

Mineral: Limestone

Gem: Freshwater pearl

Mockingbird

Iris

WHEN IT'S IRIS TIME IN TENNESSEE

Tennessee has six official state songs. This graceful waltz, honoring the official state flower, was adopted by the state legislature in 1935. Included among the other state songs are "The Tennessee Waltz" and "Rocky Top."

By Willa Mae Wald

GEOGRAPHY

Highest Point: 6,643 feet above sea level, at Clingman Dome

Lowest Point: 182 feet above sea level, in Shelby County

Area: 42,144 square miles

Greatest Distance North to South: 116 miles

Greatest Distance East to West: 482 miles

Largest Cave: Cumberland Caverns

Bordering States: Kentucky and Virginia to the north; North Carolina to the east; Georgia, Alabama, and Mississippi to the south; Arkansas and Missouri to the west

Hottest Recorded Temperature: 113 degrees Fahrenheit at Perryville on July 29 and August 9, 1930

Coldest Recorded Temperature: –32 degrees Fahrenheit at Mountain City on December 30, 1917

Average Annual Precipitation: 50 inches

Major Rivers: Big Sandy, Buffalo, Cancy Fork, Clinch, Cumberland, Duck, Elk, Forked Deer, French Broad, Harpeth, Hatchee, Hiwassee, Holston, Little Tennessee, Loosahatchie, Mississippi, Obion, Powell, Sequatchie, Stones, Tennessee, Wolf

Major Lakes: Boone, Cherokee, Chickamauga, Douglas, Fort Loudoun, Fort Patrick Henry, Norris, Pickwick, Reelfoot, Watauga, Watts Bar

Mountains: Appalachian, Bald, Blue Ridge, Chilhowee, Cumberland, Great Smoky, Holston, Iron, Roan, Stone, Unicoi, Unaka

Trees: ash, beech, cedar, cherry, cypress, elm, hickory, maple, red and white oak, shortleaf pine, sycamore, walnut, yellow poplar

Wild Plants: azalea, dragonroot, hop clover, iris, mountain laurel, rhododendron, spring beauty, yellow jasmine

Animals: beaver, black bear, bobcat, fox, muskrat, opossum, rabbit, raccoon, skunk, white squirrel, white-tailed deer, wild hog

Game Birds: Canada goose, duck, quail, wild turkey

Birds: anhinga, bald eagle, egret, hawk, heron, marten, mockingbird, owl, raven, robin

Fish: bass, catfish, crappie, rainbow trout, walleyed pike

Endangered Animals: Alabama lamp mussel, Appalachian elktoe (mussel), Bachman's warbler, Barrens darter, Carolina northern flying squirrel, cats paw (mussel), Eastern cougar, lake sturgeon, Nashville crayfish, pallid sturgeon, peregrine falcon, red wolf, red woodpecker, southern club shell (mussel)

Endangered Plants: American water pennywort, American yew, Blue Ridge goldenrod, Carolina anemone, leafed trillium, leafy prairie clover, Roan Mountain bluet, Ruth's golden aster, purple fringeless orchid, skunk cabbage, sweet fern, Tennessee coneflower, white fringeless orchid, yellow fringeless orchid

White-tailed deer

TIMELINE

c. 11,000 BC Paleo-Indians come to the Tennessee area during the last ice age.

1540 Hernando de Soto of Spain becomes the first European to explore the Tennessee region.

1673 English, Canadian, and French explorers come to the Tennessee area.

1772 East Tennessee settlers (the Watauga Association) write their own constitution.

1775 Daniel Boone helps clear the Cumberland Gap in the mountains, opening the way for pioneers to go west.

1775–1783 The American Revolution is fought.

1779 The first city in Tennessee, Jonesborough, is founded.

1784 East Tennessee breaks away from North Carolina to form its own country, the Republic of Franklin.

1790 The Territory South of the Ohio River is created.

1796 Tennessee becomes the sixteenth state and approves its first constitution.

1812 The War of 1812 breaks out between England and the United States.

1829 Andrew Jackson of Tennessee becomes president of the United States.

1834 The right to vote is taken away from free blacks.

1838 The federal government forces the Cherokee out of Tennessee (Trail of Tears).

1843 Nashville becomes the state capital.

1844 Tennessee governor James K. Polk is elected president.

1861 The Civil War begins; Tennessee is the last state to secede from (leave) the Union.

1862 The Battle of Shiloh is fought in Tennessee.

1864 The Battle of Nashville, the last major conflict fought in the state, takes place.

1865 The Civil War ends; Andrew Johnson of Tennessee becomes president after Lincoln's assassination.

1866 Tennessee becomes the first Southern state to rejoin the Union.

1870 Tennessee draws up its third constitution and gives all male citizens age twenty-one and older the right to vote.

1920 Tennessee becomes the thirty-sixth state to give women the right to vote.

1925 The Scopes "Monkey Trial" takes place in Dayton, Tennessee.

1933 Federal government creates the Tennessee Valley Authority.

1956 Tennessee begins school integration.

1964 The first African American is elected to the Tennessee legislature.

1968 Martin Luther King Jr. is assassinated in Memphis.

1982 Knoxville hosts the World's Fair.

1996 Tennessee's first African-American chief justice is appointed to the state supreme court.

1998 A devastating tornado rips through Nashville; the University of Tennessee Volunteers become national football champions, going undefeated for the season.

2000 The Rock 'n' Soul Museum opens in Memphis.

2001 The newly renovated Country Music Hall of Fame and Museum opens in Nashville.

2002 Bill Frist becomes U.S. Senate majority leader.

2005 The "Tennessee Waltz" sting operation exposes corruption in the state legislature.

Agricultural Products: cattle, corn, cotton, dairy products, fruit, hogs, lumber, poultry, sheep, soybeans, tobacco, vegetables, wheat

Manufactured Products: chemicals, clothing, electrical and electronic equipment, food processing, food products, machinery, metal products, paper products, plastic products, printed materials, rubber products, transportation equipment

Cattle

Natural Resources: ball clay, barite, coal, copper, crushed stone, fluorite, gravel, iron, lignite, limestone, marble, natural gas, petroleum, phosphate rock, pyrite, sand, zinc

Business and Trade: agriculture, banking, construction, insurance, manufacturing (including automobiles), mining, real estate, service industry, transportation, wholesale and retail trade

CALENDAR OF CELEBRATIONS

Eagle Watch Tours Every January through March, visitors can get a close-up look at the many bald eagles that make their winter home in Reelfoot Lake.

Mule Day Festival During the first week of April, Columbia celebrates its fame as the mule-raising capital of Tennessee with a mule-pulling parade, mule shows, down-home cooking, and arts and crafts.

Dogwood Arts Festival This seventeen-day festival is held every April in Knoxville to celebrate the dogwood trees in bloom in the city.

World's Biggest Fish Fry April in Paris, Tennessee, is the time for eating the best-tasting catfish, served at the fairgrounds.

Memphis in May International Festival For the entire month of May, Memphis holds plays, concerts, fairs, and the Cotton Maker's Jubilee, the largest African-American parade.

Tennessee Crafts Fair Held in the first week of May, Centennial Park in Nashville comes alive with art displays, a puppet theater, crafts demonstrations, and children's craft activities.

Tennessee Strawberry Festival The first or second week of May is when the town of Dayton has a ten-day children's fair, with sports events, a quilt show, a carnival, storytelling, and the world's longest strawberry shortcake.

Summer Lights Held at the end of May or at the beginning of June, this music festival in Nashville has bands of every kind playing on large outdoor stages.

Rhododendron Festival The middle of June brings the Rhododendron Festival to Roan Mountain, along with mountain music, dancing, food, and wildlife tours.

International Country Music Fan Fair Nashville in mid-June is when fans have a chance to meet their favorite country music stars.

Old-Time Fiddlers' Jamboree and Crafts Festival In early July country music and crafts fill the streets of Smithville, where the town holds a "fiddle-off" on the square to pick the best fiddler.

Fan Fair

Appalachian Fair For a week in mid-August, Gray, Tennessee, hosts a huge fair featuring a carnival, farm displays, tractor pulls, baking contests, entertainment, and crafts from Appalachia.

Elvis Week Mid-August in Memphis brings citywide celebrations, including a tour of Elvis's junior high school and his early recording studio.

Tennessee Walking Horse Celebration For ten days at the end of August, Shelbyville celebrates the Tennessee walking horse with a contest for choosing the National Grand Champion of the breed. A dog show and petting zoo add to the fun.

Apple Festival Held in Erwin in the fall, this celebration features music and dancing, food, crafts, a pottery show and sale, and a four-mile footrace.

Reelfoot Lake Arts and Crafts Festival Reelfoot Lake State Park hosts a large arts and crafts festival at the beginning of October.

Heritage Days Held in the fall at the home of Sam Davis, the Boy Hero of the Confederacy, this festival in Smyrna features blacksmiths, weavers, and others who show how the Davis family and their slaves lived during the Civil War.

National Storytelling Festival On the first weekend in October, the historic town of Jonesborough holds a three-day festival that brings together the best storytellers from around the world.

Autumn Gold Festival Early in October Coker Creek celebrates two types of gold: the gold found in creeks and on the leaves of the trees in the fall. The fun includes panning for gold and singing and dancing to mountain music.

Mountain Makins Festival Eastern Tennessee holds one of the state's finest crafts shows each October. Mountain music is also played to add to the fun.

Christmas in the Park The Christmas season is celebrated at Cove Lake State Park, where music, lights, and decorations brighten the holiday.

STATE STARS

Roy Acuff (1903–1992), born in Maynardville, Tennessee, earned the nickname "King of Country Music." He is best known for his hit song "The Wabash Cannonball." With his band, the Smoky Mountain Boys, Acuff made Tennessee music popular around the world. He also ran unsuccessfully for governor of Tennessee in 1948.

James Agee (1909–1955), one of the greatest southern writers, was born in Knoxville. His novel *A Death in the Family* won the first Pulitzer Prize given for both a book and the play based on it. Agee also wrote Hollywood films. His most famous is *The African Queen.*

James Agee

Lamar Alexander (1940–) was the governor of Tennessee from 1978 to 1987. He also served as the secretary of education under Ronald Reagan. In 1996 Alexander was a candidate for the Republican nomination for president.

Howard Baker (1925–), born in Huntsville, Tennessee, was both the U.S. Senate majority leader (1981–1985) and the Senate minority leader (1977–1981). Baker became famous for his vigorous role in the investigation of the Watergate scandal during the administration of President Richard Nixon. He also served as Ronald Reagan's chief of staff and was appointed ambassador to Japan in 2001.

Julian Bond (1940–) of Nashville was one of the nation's foremost civil rights leaders in the 1960s. In 1968 Bond became the first African American to have his name placed in nomination for vice president. He has served as president of the Southern Poverty Law Center and as executive chairman of the National Association for the Advancement of Colored People (NAACP).

Daniel Boone (1734–1820) was one of the first pioneers to explore the frontier regions of Tennessee and Kentucky. In 1775 Boone helped clear the Cumberland Gap in the Allegheny Mountains around Tennessee. His work paved the way for pioneers to make their way west across the Appalachians.

Dorothy Brown (1919–) was the first African-American woman in the South to practice surgery. She was also the first black woman to serve in the Tennessee legislature.

Frances Hodgson Burnett (1849–1924), author of *The Secret Garden, A Little Princess, Little Lord Fauntleroy,* and many other books and short stories, was born in England but moved to Tennessee when she was sixteen years old. She spent about half her life there.

Tracy Caulkins (1963–) began swimming at the Nashville Aquatic Club when she was eight years old and qualified for the Olympic trials when she was thirteen. In the 1984 Olympics she captained the U.S. swim team, winning three gold medals and setting an Olympic record.

Davy Crockett (1786–1836) was not "born on a mountaintop in Tennessee," as the song says, but in a log cabin near Limestone Creek. Crockett was a scout in the Creek War (1813–1814), a congressperson from Tennessee, a writer, and a soldier. He lived through the Battle of the Alamo but was shot on orders of the enemy leader. He supposedly hated being called "Davy" but is usually known by that nickname.

Sam Davis (1842–1863) of Smyrna, Tennessee, was called the Boy Hero of the Confederacy. He was hanged as a spy during the Civil War for passing secret information given to him by a Union soldier. Davis refused to reveal the name of the soldier. Before the hanging, Davis told the Confederate soldiers who had captured him that he would rather die a thousand deaths than betray a friend.

David Farragut (1801–1870) of Stony Pont, Tennessee, joined the U.S. Navy at age nine. At age twelve he was briefly in charge of a captured ship. A Civil War hero, Farragut helped the Union win the war. In 1866 he became the first U.S. admiral of the navy.

Shelby Foote (1916–2005), whom some have called the greatest historian of the U.S. Civil War, settled in Memphis in 1953. He also wrote historical fiction and became well known to the American public as the narrator of a popular series on the Civil War that ran on public television in the 1990s.

Cornelia Fort (1919–1943) of Nashville was the first American woman pilot to die in service to her country. While she was flying a plane across Texas, a male pilot tried to scare her by flying too close. Their planes collided, and she was killed.

Aretha Franklin (1942–), born in Memphis but raised in Detroit, Michigan, is known as the "First Lady of Soul." One of American music's great treasures, Franklin has had one hit song after another, including "Respect." She has been nominated for more Grammy awards than any other female singer.

Nikki (Yolande Cornelia) Giovanni (1943–) is from Knoxville. She is best known for her popular children's poetry, such as her famous collection of poems *Spin a Soft Black Song*. Some of her essays and a brief biography can be found in her book *Gemini*.

Albert Gore (1948–) is known for his strong stand on the environment. Gore has been a U.S. senator and a member of Congress from Tennessee. He was elected vice president of the United States in 1992 and 1996 and ran for president in 2000.

Amy Grant (1960–) is a singer who is best known for her Christian and pop hits. She grew up in Nashville, where she continues to record her songs. Many of them have gone gold and platinum.

Red Grooms (1937–), born in Nashville, is well known for his unusual sculptures. His artwork can be seen in modern-art museums across the United States. His *Tennessee Foxtrot Carousel*, a merry-go-round with famous Tennesseans in place of horses, is a popular attraction in Nashville.

Alex Haley (1921–1992), a famous African-American author, hailed from Henning, Tennessee. It was on the front porch of his home in Henning that the young Haley first heard his family's fascinating stories about their past. Later, he used those stories to write *Roots*, an award-winning book and television miniseries that explored the overlooked history of African Americans. Haley's search for his roots led thousands of Americans to look for theirs.

W. C. Handy (1873–1958), who lived on Beale Street in Memphis, probably introduced the blues to the public. The blues is a mix of jazz and traditional work songs. Handy's songs include "Memphis Blues" and "Beale Street Blues." His work as a composer earned him the name "Father of the Blues."

W. C. Handy

Isaac Hayes (1942–   ) was born in Covington, Tennessee (near Memphis) and was raised on a farm by his grandparents. He began working as a songwriter and is considered one of the fathers of soul music.

Sam Houston (1793–1863), though born in Virginia, lived with the Cherokee in Tennessee for several years. Like Davy Crockett, Houston lived a life of adventure. He fought with Andrew Jackson in the Creek War (1813–1814) and served as a congressperson from Tennessee and as governor of the state. Later, he moved to Texas, where he was one of the most important figures in Texas's fight for independence.

Cordell Hull (1871–1955), a native of Tennessee, is called the "Father of the United Nations." Hull was the secretary of state during World War II. After the war he helped organize the United Nations as an international peacekeeping body.

Andrew Jackson (1767–1845), the seventh president of the United States (1829–1837), served in the American Revolution at the age of thirteen. He was also a hero of the War of 1812. During his long career Jackson served as a judge, a U.S. representative, and a senator from Tennessee.

Andrew Johnson (1808–1875), who became the seventeenth president of the United States, came from a very poor family. His family moved to Tennessee in 1826. In 1864 he became Abraham Lincoln's running mate. The next year he became president when Lincoln was assassinated. In 1868 the House of Representatives impeached (brought charges against) him for his lenient attitude toward the South. The Senate decided by just one vote not to remove him from office.

Casey Jones (1864–1900), whose real name was John Luther Jones, was a railroad engineer who lived in Jackson, Tennessee. When he realized that his locomotive was about to have a head-on collision with another train, he ordered everyone else on board to jump to safety while he stayed at the controls. He died with one hand on the warning whistle and the other on the brake. Wallace Saunders, one of the men whose life he saved, wrote a ballad about him. Many people are unaware that Casey Jones was a real person, not the made-up hero of a song.

Estes Kefauver (1903–1963) was a member of the U.S. House of Representatives and then of the Senate. He became famous for his work on a Senate committee formed to fight organized crime. In 1956 he was the Democratic candidate for vice president on a ticket with Adlai Stevenson.

Martin Luther King Jr. (1929–1968) was a great American civil rights leader and the youngest person to have won the Nobel Peace Prize at that time. King was assassinated in Memphis in April 1968 while there to help the city's sanitation workers, who were on strike.

Mary Love (1823–1887) sometimes called the "Paul Revere of Tennessee," made her famous ride in November of 1863. During the Civil War Love hid a message from General Ulysses S. Grant to another Union general in her clothing. She was caught by Confederate soldiers but refused to give them any information. The soldiers never found the message and let her go.

Peyton Manning (1976–) joined the Indianapolis Colts after playing on the University of Tennessee's football team. He has received two National Football League Most Valuable Player awards, made five Pro Bowl appearances, and has twice been selected All-Pro. He is the only athlete whose number has beeen retired by the University of Tennessee.

Leroy Robert ("Satchel") Paige (1906?–1982) was a star pitcher in the Negro leagues, the all-black professional baseball leagues. Paige played for both the Nashville Elite Giants and the Chattanooga Black Look-outs. After the integration of baseball, Paige joined the Major Leagues at age forty-two. He was the first member of the Negro leagues to become a member of the Baseball Hall of Fame.

Dolly Parton (1946–), a country music superstar, was born near Sevierville. Parton is famous for her singing and acting. She is also part-owner of Dollywood, a huge musical theme park in Pigeon Forge, Tennessee.

James K. Polk (1795–1849) served as the eleventh U.S. president (1845–1849). Born in North Carolina, Polk was raised in Tennessee. He served as a member of the Tennessee legislature and the U.S. House of Representatives, where he was elected speaker. He was also the governor of Tennessee.

Elvis Presley (1935–1977), the "King of Rock 'n' Roll," was born in Mississippi but grew up and attended school in Memphis. Presley's first hits were recorded in Memphis at the tiny Sun Studios. Elvis's mansion in Memphis, Graceland, is filled with his gold records and glittering costumes and is one of the nation's most popular tourist attractions.

Ishmael Reed (1938–   ), born in Chattanooga, has used Tennessee as a setting in many of his writings. Reed is known for his poetry and fiction. Much of his writing is about the poor treatment of African Americans.

Wilma Rudolph (1940–1994), an Olympic champion, wore a leg brace as a child. She went on to become a member of the Tigerbelles, the famous women's track team at Tennessee State University. In 1960 Rudolph became the first American woman to win three gold medals in track in the Olympics.

Wilma Rudolph

Clarence Saunders (1881–1953) of Memphis invented the first supermarket. Saunders's idea for the self-service food store changed the way Americans shopped. He called his store Piggly Wiggly after seeing a pig struggling to get under a fence.

Sequoyah (1760?–1843) invented an alphabet for the Cherokee language, thereby bringing reading and writing to his people.

John Sevier (1745–1815) served as the first and only governor of the Republic of Franklin (1785–1788). In 1772 Sevier led a group of settlers (the Watauga Association) to start their own state. Franklin failed, and Sevier later became the governor of Tennessee.

Bessie Smith (1898?–1937) was born in Chattanooga and started her stage career at an early age. When she was a young woman, her talent was noticed by the great blues singer Ma Rainey, and she began singing the blues throughout the South. She moved to Philadelphia in 1920. Her recording of "Down Hearted Blues" sold over 2 million copies. She is known as the "Empress of the Blues." She died after a car accident, and some say she might have lived if she had been given treatment in a hospital that did not admit African Americans.

Nancy Ward (**Nanye-hi**) (1738–1822), nicknamed Tsistunagiska, or Cherokee Rose, was a leader of the Cherokee people. She believed in peace and often warned settlers about Cherokee attacks. When she married a white settler, Bryan Ward, she changed her first name to Nancy.

Ida B. Wells (1862–1931) was born in Mississippi, the daughter of slaves. She moved to Memphis in 1884 and was a well-known early civil rights leader. After Wells was arrested for refusing to give up her seat in a railroad car to a group of white people, she sued the railroad. Although she lost, her case led many people to understand that segregation was unfair. Wells gained even greater fame as one of America's best-known black newspaper editors.

Oprah Winfrey

Oprah Winfrey (1954–) was born in Mississippi but moved to Nashville as a teen. She began her television career at Nashville's Channel 5. Though Winfrey has starred in and produced films, her real fame has come as a popular television talk-show host. Today, she is one of the richest women in the United States.

Reese Witherspoon (1976–   ) was born in Baton Rouge, Louisiana, but her family soon moved to Nashville, where she grew up. After acting in TV ads, she was cast in the movie *The Man in the Moon* when she was fourteen years old. She has since acted in many Hollywood films.

Reese Witherspoon

Alvin C. York (1887–1964) is considered by many to be the most famous hero of World War I. Born in the Cumberland Mountains of Tennessee, Sergeant York singlehandedly defeated a group of Germans at the Battle of Argonne Forest (1918). For his bravery he received the Congressional Medal of Honor, the highest U.S. military award.

TOUR THE STATE

Andrew Johnson National Historic Site (Greeneville) The house Johnson lived in before he became president and his small tailor shop are interesting places to visit.

Davy Crockett Birthplace State Park (Limestone) A reconstruction of the tiny log cabin in which Davy Crockett was born stands where the original cabin once stood.

Rocky Mount (Piney Flats) This two-story log cabin, built in 1770, is the oldest original capital of a territory in the United States.

Cumberland Gap National Historical Park (Cumberland Gap) This 20,000-acre park is located in Tennessee, Virginia, and Kentucky, at the site where Daniel Boone cleared the Cumberland Gap, the passageway across the mountains to the West.

Great Smoky Mountain National Park (Great Smoky Mountains) Clingmans Dome, the highest point in Tennessee, and the Appalachian Trail make this park an awesome sight.

Norris Dam State Park (Norris) This park contains the Norris Dam, a product of the Tennessee Valley Authority (TVA), and the Lenoir Museum of interesting objects.

Museum of Appalachia (Norris) More than twenty-five reconstructed log cabins and thousands of real pioneer items can be found in this museum dedicated to the life and times of the Appalachian pioneer.

American Museum of Science and Energy (Oak Ridge) Hands-on displays and demonstrations teach visitors about the different kinds of energy.

Dollywood (Pigeon Forge) This large musical theme park, started by Dolly Parton, has thrilling rides, great entertainment, crafts, and shops.

Lost Sea Caverns (Sweetwater) Visitors can hike down to the world's largest underground lake (4.5 acres) and ride in a glass-bottomed boat to see unusual sea life.

Sequoyah Birthplace Museum (Vonore) The life of Sequoyah, the inventor of the Cherokee alphabet, and the history of the Cherokee people are memorialized here.

Lookout Mountain (Chattanooga) Visitors can ride the world's steepest passenger railway a mile up to the top of the mountain, from which they can view seven states!

Tennessee Aquarium (Chattanooga) The aquatic exhibit is called the "world's first major freshwater life center" and it contains 350 different kinds of fish found in the state.

Cherokee National Forest (Cleveland) This giant forest features scenic views, long hiking trails, and interesting wildlife.

Lookout Mountain Railway

Dunbar Cave State Natural Area (Clarksville) Nature walks, cave tours, and stories about the Native Americans who lived in these caves thousands of years ago are the attraction there.

Polk Ancestral Home (Columbia) Visit the historic home of one of America's least-known but hardest-working and most effective presidents.

The Old Stone Fort (Manchester) This stone fort stands in the middle of a state park. A museum gives information about the prehistoric Woodland Indians who built it.

Nashville Toy Museum (Nashville) Teddy bears, dolls, dollhouses, toy cars, trucks, boats, planes, and two working model railroads make this a great place to visit.

Nashville Zoo (Nashville) More than six hundred animals roam free there in a beautiful country setting.

Cumberland Science Museum (Nashville) This hands-on museum has traveling science shows, displays about the environment, a planetarium, and live animal demonstrations.

Music Row (Nashville) These streets in downtown Nashville contain museums featuring country music stars, recording studios, and souvenir shops.

Downtown (Nashville) Attractions include the 130,000-square-foot Country Music Hall of Fame and Museum, the Frist Center for the Visual Arts, and historic Second Avenue, with restaurants, stores, and music.

Capitol (Nashville) This beautiful building was completed in 1859, making it one of the oldest state capitols. President James K. Polk is buried inside.

Hermitage (near Nashville) Andrew Jackson, the seventh president, built and lived in this huge white home. The property also features its own church, log cabins, gardens, smokehouse, and tomb.

Shiloh National Military Park (Shiloh) The park is located on the site of one of the bloodiest battles of the Civil War.

The Alex Haley House and Museum (Henning) The porch of this house is where young Haley heard stories about his family's history, which sparked the idea behind his famous book *Roots*. Each room in the museum tells a story about Haley's life.

Casey Jones Village (Jackson) A fifteen-minute video, an 1890s railroad car, and a full-size steam locomotive give visitors a chance to learn about the famous railroad engineer memorialized in American folklore, Casey Jones.

Graceland (Memphis) The home of Elvis Presley, the "King of Rock 'n' Roll," contains fabulous mementos of the singer's life.

National Civil Rights Museum (Memphis) The story of Martin Luther King Jr. and other civil rights leaders is told in this museum, built on the site of King's assassination.

Children's Museum of Memphis (Memphis) Young visitors can crawl through a tree house, climb an eight-story skyscraper, sit in a wheelchair, "drive" a real car, and simply have fun.

Peabody Hotel (Memphis) A duck parade twice a day from the lobby to the fountain of the hotel is one of the most popular attractions in Memphis.

Chucalissa Museum (Memphis) A reconstructed Native American village at the University of Memphis gives visitors an accurate picture of Native American life before the coming of white settlers.

Mississippi River Museum (Mud Island) Visiting this museum is a good way to learn about the history of the Mississippi River and the people who made their homes near it.

Reelfoot Lake State Resort Park (Tiptonville) Formed by a tremendous earthquake, this large park has boating, a wildlife refuge, a duck-calling contest, eagle watch tours, and an arts and crafts festival in October.

FUN FACTS

The world's only guitar-shaped music museum can be found in Bristol, Tennessee.

Kenton, Tennessee is home to two hundred albino squirrels claimed to be left by a Gypsy caravan in 1869.

Find Out More

Would you like to learn more about Tennessee? Look for the following titles in your library, bookstore, or video store, or on the Internet.

BOOKS

Alphin, Elaine Marie and Tim Parlin. *Davy Crockett*. Minneapolis, MN: Lerner, 2002.

Barrett, Tracy. *The Trail of Tears: An American Tragedy*. Logan, IA: Perfection Learning Corporation, 2000.

Kent, Deborah. *Tennessee*. Danbury, CT: Children's Press, 2001.

McClellan, Adam. *Uniquely Tennessee*. Portsmouth, NH: Heinemann, 2003.

Shoulders, Michael. *Discover Tennessee: Two Great Ways to Discover the Volunteer State!* Farmington Hills, MI: Thomson Gale, 2004.

Sirvaitis, Karen. *Tennessee*. Minneapolis, MN: Lerner Publications, 2002.

Weatherly, Myra S. *Tennessee*. Danbury, CT: Children's Press, 2001.

The State of Tennessee

www.k-12.state.tn.us/weblinks/ShowMeResource.asp

This site for students leads you to resources and popular sites on the State of Tennessee. Select a report and click on "Generate List."

Tennessee Blue Book

www.state.tn.us/sos/bluebook/online/bbonline.htm

The state's "Blue Book" gives facts about the Tennessee government, history, state symbols, and more.

Tennessee Government

www.tennessee.gov

This is the official Web site of the State of Tennessee.

Tennessee Encyclopedia

http://tennesseeencyclopedia.net/

This is the online version of *The Tennessee Encyclopedia of History and Culture*.

Tennessee Historical Society

www.tennesseehistory.org

This is the Web site of the Tennessee State Historical Society.

Index

Page numbers in **boldface** are illustrations and charts.

ABOUT THE AUTHOR

Tracy Barrett is the author of numerous fiction and nonfiction books for young readers. Tracy holds an A.B. from Brown University and an M.A. and Ph.D. from the University of California at Berkeley. She has been married to Greg Giles since 1983 and has two children: Laura Beth, twenty-one, and Patrick, eighteen. She lives in Nashville, Tennessee, where she teaches at Vanderbilt University. Visit her at www.tracybarrett.com.